GST HANDBOOK

The Financial Post

GST HANDBOOK

A PRACTICAL GUIDE FOR BUSINESS

SAMUEL SLUTSKY

KEY PORTER BOOKS

Canadian Cataloguing in Publication Data

Slutsky, Samuel
The Financial post GST primer

ISBN 1-55013-261-X

1. Goods and services tax – Canada.* I. Title.
HJ5715.C3S5 1990 343.7105'52 C90-094372-6

Key Porter Books Limited
70 The Esplanade
Toronto, Ontario
M5E 1R2

Typesetting: Pixel Graphics, Inc.

Printed and bound in Canada

90 91 92 93 94 95 6 5 4 3 2 1

To Gloria

Contents

Disclaimer

I. Introduction

It is anticipated that the proposed Goods and Services Tax will become law on January 1, 1991. Although the Canadian Senate intends to study the legislation before allowing it to pass into legislation, it is doubtful that delays will result in delayed implementation of the GST Bill. Revenue Canada is currently preparing for January 1 implementation and could conceivably accommodate that process even if the bill were held up until December 31.

A multi-stage tax was first proposed by Finance Minister Michael Wilson in the June 18, 1987 White Paper on Tax Reform. The proposals, which began in earnest in 1985, were based on consultations with the public. The government had come to the end of the rope with proposals respecting the flawed federal sales tax. It was finally considered that the manufacturer's tax had to be replaced with a new and viable system that would remove the fundamental flaws that the existing system introduced into the business world.

The most important thing to note about GST is that it represents a change to the tax system in this country of a magnitude that has not been experienced since 1917, when the Income War Tax Act was introduced as a temporary measure. It will affect most of the businesses in Canada to a degree that was never reached under the federal sales tax system. It will be visible and all-inclusive.

Business will have to accommodate the new system by understanding that it will change how day-to-day operations are conducted. New strategies and objectives will have to be developed to accommodate these changes. Those who don't rise to the challenge of integrating the tax with existing operations will lose money — pure and simple. It is therefore critical that business come to grips with GST as soon as possible.

The final form of the GST Bill (C-62) was passed by the House of Commons on April 18, 1990. This book was based on that draft legislation. Note that the commentary reflects the Quick Accounting Method that was announced on May 31, 1990, by Otto Jelinek, the Minister of National Revenue. It also addresses the federal sales tax inventory rebate percentages announced on June 1, 1990, by Michael Wilson, the Minister of Finance.

II. GST: An Overview

The GST is a multi-stage sales tax that applies to every commercial transaction in the supply chain, up to and including retail sales. However, commercial operations, with some limited exceptions, are able to recover the tax.

There is one real difference between GST and all of the other tax systems that consumers have experienced — the taxation of services at the point of sale. Up to now, tax systems, both federal income tax and sales tax, as well as provincial sales taxes, have not imposed a direct tax on services. Consumers are not used to paying tax for a haircut, shoeshine or to get their grass cut. Nor have they paid tax to have a will prepared or have their income tax returns completed by an accountant.

That's all going to change under GST.

The GST is also going to be fundamentally different for Canadian businesses. Up to now, taxes on goods have always been treated as a cost. In most situations, federal sales tax is not recoverable.

The GST doesn't work that way. Rather, taxpayers carrying on business, whether as corporations, trusts, partnerships or sole proprietors (your corner grocer) will be able to recover all of the GST they pay on supplies they have to buy to provide their goods and services to customers. This recovery is accomplished by allowing suppliers a credit for tax they have paid against the taxes they must collect and remit on sales. For example, a manufacturer pays $70 of GST to buy $1,000 of material to produce shirts. On their sale to a retailer for $3,000, the manufacturer collects $210 of GST. Since the manufacturer paid $70 of GST on its purchases, only $140 will have to be paid to the government.

The system allows the manufacturer to recover the $70 of tax "inputs" from taxes collected "outputs." In this way, all of the taxes paid to produce the goods is passed on to the next commercial level.

Only consumers who pay retail prices for the goods will not be able to recover GST by "passing it on" to someone else. The retailers who sell the shirts are able to recover the $210 they paid to the manufacturer out of the GST collected from consumers on their sales.

Since a multi-stage sales tax was first proposed by the June 18, 1987 White Paper on Tax Reform, it has been clear that a few exceptions to the tax would be allowed. Numerous industry groups have energetically lobbied the Minister of Finance either for or against exceptions, with mixed results. All of the lobbies addressed the technique that would be used to implement the exceptions. Three options were available, including the "exemption," "zero-rating" and "full-taxation" methods.

Under an exemption method, a supplier pays tax on purchases, and does not charge tax on sales. Thus, tax is not directly recovered from the system. The only way an exempt purchaser can recover the GST is indirectly, by raising prices to its customers. A hidden tax burden is passed on. Under this method, the supplier effectively becomes a consumer of tax. Like the old federal sales tax, it becomes a cost of doing business.

Alternatively, under a zero-rating method, the supplier pays tax on its purchase and notionally charges tax on sales, but at a rate of zero. This entitles the supplier to a credit for input taxes.

The method usually has the least impact on the parties in a

supply chain in practical terms. The government is the only loser because tax is not collected on sales by zero-rated suppliers and the GST paid by them is recoverable.

Finally, with a full taxation method, all sales are completely subject to tax and the supplier is entitled to recover input taxes. The purchaser then retrieves the tax by way of a tax rebate scheme.

This method really looks and works like the regular GST system. However, a separate refund mechanism is established to allow the purchaser in the supply chain to recover taxes paid. Foreign tourists, for example, will be beneficiaries of a full taxation system by being able to obtain refunds of GST after they leave the country.

Of the three methods of excepting goods and services from the new system, the "exemption" method carries the potential to impose a non-recoverable tax burden on a supplier. It allows a consumer to obtain the goods or services free of GST, but does not grant the supplier a corresponding credit for the taxes incurred to provide them.

The government will use this method to except various services from the new system, including residential rents, health and dental services (including hospital and nursing homes), daycare and education services, as well as legal aid services.

For example, where a dentist provides tax-free services to a patient, the cost of providing those services will be increased by the GST paid for rent, equipment, supplies and other overheads. This could result in as much as a 7% cost increase, depending on how those services are delivered.

Businesses providing exempted services might consider several recovery methods. For example, they could pass on the additional cost of the tax to consumers by raising prices. While this could work easily for non-regulated industries (such as dentistry) where legal restrictions are not imposed on the increase, it will be much more difficult for regulated sectors, such as health services.

Doctors will find that their costs rise by the GST paid for their overheads. At the same time, they won't be able to pass the additional costs on to provincial health insurance plans, which on paying medical fees only allow claims based on regulated fee schedules. In these circumstances, the imposition of an exemption method will represent a substantial increase in costs to medical practitioners in private practice.

While certain public sector institutions providing exempt services, such as universities, will be given direct rebates to lighten the burden of providing tax-exempt services, the rebates will only partially recoup the additional taxes.

The only major cost component of doing business that is not subject to GST are employee costs. GST is not payable on salaries and wages.

In contrast, GST has to be paid on independent labour costs, such as those supplied by independent contractors. Up to now, using sub-contracted labour, rather than hiring employees to complete the work, has been a business decision. Under GST, the tax burden will have to be taken into account. For taxable suppliers, the decision won't be difficult. They will be able to recover the tax in the ordinary course of events. The same can be said for zero-rated businesses.

Exempt suppliers are in a different position. Every dollar of GST paid means an additional dollar of cost that can only be recovered by raising prices to buyers. Exempt businesses will have a vested interest to save GST by hiring employees to complete tasks that were formerly done by independent contractors. For example, financial institutions will, for many of their services, be considered exempt taxpayers. As a result, they will be inclined to hire employees in areas such as legal and accounting services, where they would previously have hired independent firms to do the work.

III. GST: Daily Operations

1. Registration

Business will be stampeding to register under the GST because of the enormous cash benefits of doing so. Those who don't register as soon as possible are only hurting themselves.

Revenue Canada believes there will be between 1.5 and 2 million registrants under the system when it is mature. It is expected that over a million of the registrants will fit into the small business category (annual sales of between $30,000 and $500,000).

Registration forms were first mailed to potential registrants in the spring of 1990. The registration package included basic information and a one-page form.

Revenue Canada is particularly proud of that form. It could easily have been ten pages long. Instead, the Department worked day and night for months, consulted with the public, and pared down the information required to the absolute essentials. The objective was to make registration a painless process.

Registrants who complete forms are provided with more detailed information packages to help with implementation and operation under the system. In some ways, the additional information is available as an incentive to sign up early.

The fascinating thing about the registration process is that it is completely voluntary. Until the GST becomes law, Canadians have no legal liability to comply with any of the proposals, including registration. While some might see this as an opportunity to delay acceptance of the new system, failure to register could cost them a lot.

Registration is critical for two very important reasons. They include:

- Receiving the federal sales tax inventory rebate. Only registrants under GST will be allowed to apply for a cash refund of the federal sales tax content of inventories (see Chapter V for more details) owned as at the GST implementation date. Businesses registered before January 1, 1991, will be able to file for the refund immediately on the GST start-up date. Those who have not registered after that date may not be entitled to apply for the refund.
- Recovery of GST paid on purchases. Everything purchased by businesses after December 31, 1990, will be subject to GST. Though input tax credits can be recovered immediately, they won't be available to non-registrants. Every day inputs are not recovered will mean extra financing costs (i.e., interest on debt borrowed to pay for input taxes). If cash flows, rather than debt, are used to finance input taxes, then lost time in recovery will mean lost profits from cash that could otherwise be earning interest for the business.

Another reason for registering early is the rebate offered to small business to help upgrade cash register equipment. Up to $1,000 will be available in this regard only after a business has registered (see Chapter III, "Rebates," for a discussion of this incentive).

The registration process will have two stages. The first stage will be on implementation of the GST, at which point all business, other than those which qualify as "small suppliers" — less than $30,000 in annual sales (see Chapter III, "Small Business Suppliers") — will be expected to sign up.

The second stage will continue after implementation, when small suppliers grow and their sales exceed the $30,000 threshold. Once surpassed, small suppliers will have the legal obligation to register under GST.

Small suppliers who become registrants after the initial phase will be entitled to an immediate input tax credit for supplies and equipment on hand at the date of registration. Thus, they will be able to recover any GST paid on supplies or equipment used in their business on hand at that time.

Small supplier registrants will be entitled to the lesser of two amounts. The first is the actual GST paid in relation to those supplies and equipment. If the GST cannot be determined, the second amount is tax that the supplier would have been required to pay had the asset been acquired for its fair market value at the time of registration.

In these circumstances, it will normally be better for a small supplier to pursue the actual GST paid in relation to the assets on which the input credit is claimed. At the time registration is made, the fair market value of the asset may have dropped below its actual cost (a normal event for many supplies and equipment). Therefore, if the fair market value standard is used, the input credits may be quite a bit less than the actual GST that was paid on their original purchase.

For example, assume that a carpenter who qualifies as a small supplier purchases a lathe for $7,000 and pays $490 in GST while a small supplier in 1991. In 1992, sales having been good, and having exceeded the $30,000 threshold, the carpenter is obligated to become a registrant. At that time, the lathe may only be worth $3,500 (the price someone would pay for a used machine at the time of registration). The input tax credit on registration in these circumstances would only be $245.

Since a small supplier may not know at the beginning of a

taxation year whether the $30,000 threshold will be exceeded in the year, it may be wise to keep track of the GST actually paid for supplies and equipment purchased in order to avoid the possible erosion of input tax credits that will be available once registration is necessary.

An attempt should also be made to claim the replacement value of the supplies and equipment as the proper foundation for the input credit calculation on the basis that when the supplies and equipment are being used in a commercial process, their fair market value to the small supplier is their replacement value. It will be up to Revenue Canada to dispute fair market valuations on this basis.

No input tax credits will be available in these situations in respect of assets that GST was never paid on. This would include, for example, supplies and equipment purchased before implementation of the GST system.

Special rules have also been provided for the recovery of GST that is paid for services or for rental property by a small supplier that becomes a registrant. In these circumstances, small suppliers will be able to claim input tax credits in respect of the cost of services or rent paid in relation to a period that commences after the supplier became a registrant. For example, assume a freelance journalist registers under the system on June 15. Rent paid for a business office on June 1 for the entire month can be pro-rated for 15 days. GST for the last 15 days of the month can be recovered as an input credit.

Note that input credits will not be available for rental charges or services provided for any period during which the small supplier was not a registrant under the system. The small supplier also has to show that the service or rent charges were incurred for consumption, use or supply in the course of the supplier's commercial activity.

In many cases, small suppliers who are registrants will experience sales below the $30,000 threshold and decide to de-register themselves under the system. De-registrations will also occur when business operations of any size are wound up. In these situations, the suppliers will have enjoyed the recovery of GST through input tax credits in respect of the supplies and equipment on hand at the date of de-registration. It would be unfair to allow de-registering suppliers to retain those tax-free assets without, in some way, imposing tax on them at the time. Without this mechanism, suppliers would have an incentive to buy as many assets as possible prior to de-registration in order to avoid the imposition of non-recoverable GST after that time.

Rules have therefore been established to deem the de-registrant to have disposed of those assets and equipment at the time they ceased to be registrants and to have collected GST on their fair market value at the time. In these circumstances, the small supplier will have an incentive to argue that the fair market value of the assets is their depreciated value, in order to avoid repaying the full GST that was paid on the initial purchase of the asset for its full cost.

Similar rules are established to recapture the GST paid and recovered as an input tax credit in relation to services and the cost of rental properties that were paid while the supplier was a registrant. Again, the GST liability will be in respect of the cost of services provided and rent paid for that period after which the supplier has ceased to be a registrant.

Note that registration will apply to any enterprise that is engaged in commercial activities. This will include non-profit organizations, like charities, clubs and churches. It will also include non-residents in certain circumstances. Therefore, commercial and other enterprises should not think themselves exempted from the system simply because they are not liable for income or other sales taxes.

Any persons engaged in a "commercial activity" will be required to register under the legislation. Commercial activity is defined to include any business or adventure in the nature of trade (i.e., an isolated business transaction) as well as the supply of real property. It does not include persons making exempt supplies, activities that are not carried on with a reasonable expectation of profit, or activities that are performed in relation to an office or employment.

Applications for registration have to be made within 30 days from the day on which a taxable supply in Canada was first made.

Several types of people will not have to register. These include small suppliers (as noted above), non-residents who don't carry on business in Canada and persons who sell real property otherwise than in the course of a business.

Non-residents that solicit orders by mail or courier for prescribed goods (determined by regulation) will be considered to be carrying on business in Canada and will have to register and remit GST. This will apply in the case of magazines, periodicals and books delivered by mail or courier from outside the country. A transitional rule is established to exempt subscriptions to periodicals from GST where they are paid before 1991. Note that non-residents who carry on business but don't have a permanent establishment in Canada will have to post security for their GST outputs. Non-residents will, however, be entitled to input credits in the ordinary course (see Chapter III, "Non-Residents," for more detail).

Revenue Canada will issue registration numbers to applicants and confirm, in writing, the effective date of registration. The Department can also revoke registration in certain circumstances.

Revocation can occur where the Department considers that the person no longer needs to be registered or where a small supplier requests that registration be revoked. Written notice will be sent in these situations confirming the cancellation and its effective date.

2. Small Suppliers — Less Than $30,000 in Sales

Complying with the GST is going to cost money and time — two things which many small businesses do not have in abundance. The government was sensitive to this consideration and in designing the GST system, established a "small supplier" category of business which can, if it chooses, stay opted out of the tax. The real issue is whether opting out of the tax is a good thing.

Unlike other tax systems, the GST has built-in incentives for businesses to be fully taxable. It is only in this way that the tax does not represent a cost, but rather a cash flow item. If a business is fully taxable, then it can recover all of the GST it pays in the normal course of operations. If a business is not taxable, however, then it doesn't recover any GST paid on purchases.

Small suppliers will not be taxable under GST. They will not have to charge GST on sales. At the same time, they will not be entitled to claim input credits in respect of GST paid on purchases during the course of business.

So when is it a good idea to be a small supplier ?

Where the supplier sells products predominantly to purchasers who are registered under the GST (i.e., commercial enterprises), it will probably not be a good idea to claim the small supplier status. The purchasers will want these purchases to be taxable, so they can claim input tax credits and recover the tax.

Thus, for example, freelance journalists will probably want to avoid the small supplier status because the papers and magazines they write for will want to claim input tax credits for, what represents to them, a significant cost of producing their products.

Where supplies are not taxable, it usually means that the purchaser is paying for a hidden GST component that cannot be recovered as an input tax credit. Taxable purchasers will therefore always be looking for taxable suppliers and the system provides them with an incentive to avoid small suppliers who are not registered.

This factor will provide small suppliers with an incentive to be registered.

Where sales by suppliers are predominantly to non-commercial users (i.e., consumers), vendors might want small supplier status in order to reduce the selling price of their goods. While the small supplier will treat GST incurred on purchases of supplies and services as a cost in these circumstances, these inputs can be recovered by raising prices to consumers. However, this price increase can be quite a lot less than the cost of imposing a full 7% on the gross purchase price of a product, especially where the greatest part of that cost relates to services.

For example, assume a dressmaker buys $50 worth of materials (paying $3.50 in GST) to make a dress which is to be sold for $250. Adding the $3.50 to the $250 purchase price would result in a total selling price of $253.50.

Alternatively, if the dressmaker was to register under the system, the $3.50 could be directly recovered as an input tax credit. However, on the sale of the dress at $250, the consumer would have to pay an additional $17.50, for a difference of $14. In either case, the dressmaker would realize the same profits on the sale.

In order to keep prices competitive, the dressmaker would therefore be better off retaining a small supplier status and avoiding the price increase that would be associated with registration under the system.

The small supplier status is available to any business, whether or not a sole proprietorship, with sales that do not exceed $30,000. It's important to keep in mind how the $30,000 threshold is determined.

The specific rule states that the status will be available throughout any calendar quarter (i.e., January to March, April to June, July to September and October to December) and the immediately following month if the gross receipts collected on taxable transactions in the preceding 12-month period did not exceed $30,000.

This provides a continuously revolving determination based on sales in a previous period that is balanced on three months of sales. It has the effect of causing a small supplier to lose that status more quickly than a determination based on a preceding taxation year or other fiscal period.

For example, assume that a plumber with small supplier

status has sales of $5,000 per quarter for each quarter period in 1991 (for total 1991 sales of $20,000). In the second quarter of 1992 (i.e., April to June), extraordinary sales of $25,000 are experienced.

The plumber would lose entitlement to the small supplier status in the third quarter of 1992 (i.e., the July to September period). That is the first time that the sales for the preceding 12-month period exceeded the $30,000 threshold. The calculation would be as follows:

Second Quarter of 1992	Sales = $25,000
First Quarter of 1992	Sales = $ 5,000
Fourth Quarter of 1991	Sales = $ 5,000
Third Quarter of 1991	Sales = $ 5,000
Total	$40,000

Small suppliers will have to carefully watch their previous 12-month period sales in each quarter (and for the month following) to make sure they don't inadvertently miss an obligation to be registered when sales for the period exceed their threshold.

By the same token, when the threshold has been exceeded because of extraordinary sales, registrants will be able to work back towards eligibility for small supplier status when sales continue their normal course.

Continuing the example shown above, assume that the plumber began to experience normal sales activity of $5,000 per quarter after the extraordinary sales of $25,000 in the second quarter of 1992. In these circumstances, small supplier status would become available again in the third quarter of 1993. At that time, the previous 12-month period would no longer include the extraordinary sales experienced in the second quarter of 1992, and total sales for that period would be $20,000, well below the $30,000 threshold.

Several ancillary rules have to be kept in mind when calculating the threshold. First of all, the $30,000 in sales is determined without reference to sales of capital property. Thus, if a carpenter sells a lathe, the proceeds will not be included in his taxable sales for the purposes of this determination.

Secondly, the threshold will be calculated on taxable sales of the small supplier and any associated person (defined to include associated corporations and their controlling shareholders, as well as members of partnerships). Without this type of rule, one taxpayer could create dozens of corporations or other business vehicles which could each claim the small supplier status for their particular area of sales, circumventing the requirement to be registered where sales exceed the threshold.

A special rule exists for persons involved in lottery or gambling businesses who earn prize winnings. These winnings will not be counted for the purposes of determining the threshold.

Finally, limitations are placed on non-residents who sell admission to places of amusement, seminars or similar activities or events. This will cause GST to be charged on the price of admission to these events even though the total proceeds collected by the non-resident is less than $30,000.

3. Liability for GST

Legally, purchasers are liable to pay the 7% GST on all of the taxable supplies they buy. Vendors act as collection agents for the government and do not have a primary liability for the tax.

In real terms, sellers or vendors in the market place will be responsible for charging and collecting GST on their sales. They also have a primary responsibility to remit GST to the government.

Special rules are enacted that consider GST to have been collected by a vendor at the time the taxable transaction is deemed to occur (i.e., generally the date of payment or the date payment becomes legally due), triggering a liability to remit the tax.

The problem is that this liability arises and remittances must be made even though the purchaser hasn't actually paid for the goods or services. That can leave the vendor in a very precarious position.

For example, assume that a retailer sells merchandise to customers on account for $1,000 which gives rise to a $70 GST tax liability. The retailer remits the $70 to the government the next month and waits for payment from its customers.

Unfortunately, the customers don't pay and the retailer has a bad debt for the $1,000. The retailer also has a bad debt for the $70 GST it remitted to the government on behalf of the customers.

This system is really advantageous for the government. The retailer pays the tax up front and finances the $70 throughout the period that it awaits payment of its accounts. When the debt becomes bad, the retailer is out of pocket for the actual cost of the merchandise, plus the GST that has been remitted to satisfy the notional tax liability of its customers.

In order to avoid any unfairness, however, a bad debt rule is established which effectively allows the retailer to recover the $70 of GST previously remitted for the customers. Should the bad debt ever be wholly or partially recovered, the registrant would have to remit a proportionate amount in respect of the GST that was recovered.

The purchaser is not, however, off the hook simply because the retailer has written the debt off as bad. Legally, the government would be in a position to sue the deficient purchaser for the GST that should have been paid on the transaction. It can be expected that Revenue Canada will pursue its rights where the amount of GST liability is significant.

Alternatively, vendors are given the right to sue customers who owe them GST which has previously been remitted to the government. This rule allows the vendor to treat the amount as a debt and to sue the customer on that basis.

The big issue facing vendors relates to receivables. Vendors will have to remit tax to the government in many cases before the GST is actually collected from customers. Vendors will also have to finance this remittance until the tax is recovered. This is in addition to financing the cost of input taxes until they too can be recovered from GST collected or by way of refund. If this process is not managed properly, vendors can see their interest and other carrying costs soar under GST (see Chapter VI, "Cash Flows," for more details).

When does a purchaser become liable to pay GST?

GST becomes payable on the earlier of the date the payment for the taxable supply is made, or the day on which the payment becomes due.

Special rules are established for determining the day a payment will be considered to have come "due" for this purpose. In general, it will be considered to be the earliest of four days:

- The day actual payment for the supply is made.
- The earlier of the day the vendor issued an invoice, or the date on that invoice. Vendors will have to be careful to ensure that the date on the invoice and the date it was issued are the same. If they don't, they could find that the GST liability arose in a previous reporting period and that interest is charged on their delinquent remittances to the government.
- The day that the vendor would have issued an invoice, but for an undue delay on the vendor's part in doing so. This rule will limit the ability of vendors to delay a GST liability (which they might want to do to avoid having to remit tax before they are paid by a purchaser) by not issuing invoices on time; and
- The day on which a purchaser (or recipient) is legally required to give partial or whole consideration for the supply under a written agreement regarding the transaction. This deals with situations where invoices are not issued at all.

Note that this determination is critical for vendors. Their obligation to remit the tax is based on the day the liability for GST arises. Thus, they are the ones who have to determine this date for the purposes of meeting their remittance obligations.

Where they make mistakes that delay remittance past the

time that the liability arose, they will be liable to interest and penalties.

Where GST is payable in respect of a written lease agreement (whether for the supply of goods, services or rental accommodations) the tax will be payable on the same day as the lease payments fall due under the lease. It does not matter that invoices or notices of payment have been issued to a lessee before that time.

Where barter transactions take place, the items that are traded will be considered to be payment for the goods or services received in return.

Barter transactions can be tricky. Each of the parties to the transaction is supplying either goods or services as a vendor, in addition to being a purchaser that pays valuable consideration for the payment in kind. Therefore, each of the parties will be considered to have provided a supply in respect of which GST is payable. In the end, both parties to a barter transaction will have to remit GST to the government in respect of the fair market value of the goods or services bartered, determined at the time of the barter.

An exception is established for similar properties that are acquired by registrants as inventory for use exclusively in commercial activities. In these circumstances, GST does not have to be paid. This rule will facilitate certain industry practices, such as those found in the up-stream oil and gas industry, where similar products are continuously exchanged.

Where partial payments are made for a supply, or they fall due on more than one day (i.e., property supplied on a hire-purchase basis) GST will be payable separately in respect of value of each payment. The tax liability will exist on the earlier of the day the partial payment is made, or the day it becomes legally due.

Goods or services that are supplied on a continuous basis, like electricity and natural gas, will be subject to the general timing rules. Thus, as a practical matter, GST liability will arise on the earlier of the date the supplier has issued an invoice, or the date on the invoice. This will apply where the commodity is continuously supplied by way of wire, pipeline or other conduit and the supplier invoices the purchaser regularly.

In the case of real property (see Chapter IV, "Real Estate," for discussion of this topic), GST will be liable on the earlier of the date of closing (when legal title is transferred to the owner) or the date of possession.

For condominium units, the liability will arise only when registration of title occurs, regardless of the fact that possession is taken before hand. Alternatively, tax is payable 60 days after registration of title to the owner, regardless of the fact that possession has not yet been taken.

Special problems arise where the purchase price of goods or services cannot be ascertained fully at the time of sale. An example is found in the entertainment industry, where the distributor agrees to pay the owner of a motion picture film a fixed base amount, plus a percentage of admission receipts.

In these situations, GST will be payable in respect of the ascertainable portion of the price (i.e., the fixed base amount) on the day that it is paid or becomes payable by way of agreement. The balance would become payable on the day on which any part of the unascertained portion of the purchase price becomes ascertainable.

This last rule is a bit tricky. It is difficult to tell when an unascertainable amount becomes known. For example, would the admission-based percentage portion of the purchase price of a motion picture film become ascertainable after the distributor's internal auditor has counted the night's receipts? Probably not. As a practical matter, the amount would probably become ascertainable for GST purposes on the date the vendor was formally advised of the amount (such as by way of letter with cheque enclosed).

Holdbacks, such as those commonly found in the construction industry, will be subject to GST on the earlier of the day it is paid or the day the holdback period expires. This rule will only apply, however, where the holdback is sanctioned by legislation or agreed in a written contract for the construction, renovation or repair to a marine vessel or real property. In all other cases, GST will become payable on the full purchase price, in accordance with the general rule, regardless of any amounts that are held back.

In some cases, vendors will provide a combination of service, personal property and/or real property to a purchaser for an all-inclusive purchase price. To deal with the allocation of GST between the different forms of supply, a unique rule has been established. This rule is necessary to determine the time of supply for the purposes of the special rules governing significant delays by vendors in issuing invoices, as well as the time at which real property has been sold. In these situations, if the value of one of the elements of the supply is greater that the value of each of the other elements of the supply taken individually, the entire supply will be treated as a supply of the element with the higher value. For example, an appliance dealer sells kitchen cabinets with installation for an all-inclusive price. While the cabinets might be delivered in due course, it could take some time before they were installed. Under the rule, since the cabinets would clearly be more expensive than the installation costs, the entire sale would be treated as the supply of personal property.

Finally, where deposits are provided in relation to a taxable sale, GST will not be payable until the deposit is applied against the consideration owing for the supply. The exception to this rule is that tax will be payable where deposits are forfeited. The GST to be remitted will be equal to 7/107ths of the amount that is forfeited.

A concept that is critical to GST liability is the concept of "supply." A supply is defined to include any activities under which property is transferred, leased or rented, as well as any services provided whether separately or in relation to another supply (i.e., installation of a dishwasher as part of the cost of the dishwasher). Only supplies that are made in Canada will be treated as a taxable event for GST purposes. Special rules are established to determine when this condition is satisfied (see Chapter III, "Non-Residents," for details).

Entering into agreements to provide goods or services will be treated as a supply at the time the agreement is executed. GST will be liable in respect of prepayments or partial payments for a supply even where the supply has not been furnished (i.e., goods delivered or services performed) at the time payment is made. Once provided, the goods and services will be considered to be part of the same supply.

A supply will not be considered to take place where property is transferred under a security arrangement in relation to a debt. Reconveyance of the property after the debt is repaid will also not be treated as a taxable supply for GST purposes.

Where public service bodies make supplies of services or the use of a copyright, trademark, trade name or similar property to a sponsor, GST will not be liable on the basis that a taxable supply has not been made. This will cover situations where a local baseball team agrees to advertise the name of a corporate sponsor on their uniforms. This exception will not apply, however, where payments made by a sponsor are primarily made to obtain advertising on radio, television, or in newspapers, magazines or periodicals.

For greater certainty, one rule confirms tax liability in relation to leases, licences, rentals or similar arrangements for the use or right to use real property or tangible personal property. The GST relates to payment for access and enjoyment of the underlying property.

Where a taxable supply is incidental to a non-taxable supply (i.e., a prize in a box of Crackerjack), GST will not be payable in respect of the taxable supply.

Club memberships are subject to GST. Buying securities, like bonds or shares, is not. When club memberships are sold through a method that requires the purchaser to buy a share or other security in the club, the entire transaction will be considered to be a taxable supply.

Finally, a global rule is established for the receipt of supplies that are used partially in commercial activities and partially in non-commercial activities. Where substantially all of the supply is used in a taxable activity, GST inputs will be recoverable. Conversely, where substantially all of the supply is used in non-commercial (i.e., personal or exempt) activities, inputs cannot be claimed. For this purpose, the expression "substantially all" is defined to mean 90% or more.

4. Remitting GST to the Government

a. General Considerations

As a general rule, GST collected by vendors is, by law, held in trust for Her Majesty in Right of Canada — the federal government. Authority is provided, however, which allows vendors to deduct input tax credits or other deductions from these trust funds.

Remittances are made in relation to accounting periods, for which returns must be filed. Basically, remittances are due when returns are due.

Keep in mind that instalments of GST are required for small business vendors and that return based remittances may, in some cases, only represent the accounting documents that keep track of the tax that has already been remitted by way of instalments.

Vendors who, as registrants, are required to file GST returns, will be obligated to report their "net tax" for the accounting period that is covered by the return. Where the net tax amount is positive, the vendor will be required to remit the amount. The remittance must be made no later than the last day for filing the return in question (see Chapter III, "Reporting GST" for exact reporting dates).

On the other hand, where the vendor's net tax is a negative amount for the accounting period, the return will represent an application to Revenue Canada to recover the negative amount as a refund.

A vendor's net tax is a defined term. It includes all GST collected or which became collectible during the particular accounting period covered by the return. It also includes any other amounts, such as refunds of tax from suppliers, that are required to be remitted as part of the net tax for the period.

Note that amounts "collected or collectible" refers to the time at which the purchaser's liability for the tax arises (see Chapter III, "Liability for GST," for a discussion of this issue).

Net tax is reduced by input tax credits (see Chapter III, "Input Tax Credits," for details) that the vendor is entitled to claim for GST which the vendor paid, or that was considered payable, for the period covered by the return, or for a period preceding that covered by the return. It is also reduced by other amounts that the vendor is entitled to deduct from tax for that period, such as amounts written off as bad debts.

Double counting is prevented by a rule that prohibits including GST reported as collected or collectible for a previous reporting period (or an addition to net tax) in a return for any later reporting period.

A vendor's net tax is basically the difference between GST that has been collected or is collectible and the GST that has been paid or is payable as an input tax credit.

For example, assume that a wholesaler pays $100,000 in GST during the month of May on its purchases and collects $250,000 of GST during that month on sales. It will be entitled to subtract the $100,000 as an input tax credit from the $250,000 collected and be obligated to report and remit the balance, $150,000, as its net tax amount.

This is probably one of the most important aspects of the GST system. It allows vendors to recover their input taxes directly from the GST collected on sales. In theory, this aspect goes a long way towards solving some of the cash-flow problems inherent in the process. As long as vendors collect more GST than they pay, they will be able to recover input taxes immediately and not have to finance their cost.

Real predicaments occur, however, where the GST component of a sale remains a receivable past the time when vendors must remit the tax. In these circumstances, vendors have to finance the GST remittances as well as their input taxes. The GST gives vendors a 7%-plus incentive in addition to the usual cash-flow considerations to collect receivables as soon as possible.

Several restrictions are placed on determining input tax credit claims. To avoid multiple deductions of the same credit, input taxes or deductions from net tax in a return for one reporting period cannot be claimed in subsequent returns. Furthermore, an input tax credit cannot be claimed in a period where the GST became refundable or was otherwise recoverable by the vendor under another rule in the system, or under any other Act of Parliament before the end of that reporting period.

Where the supply of a residential complex is exempt because the vendor has not claimed an input tax credit in respect of the complex (see Chapter IV, "Real Estate"), it will be prohibited from claiming a credit in respect of those input taxes after the exempt supply has been made.

Note that input taxes can be carried forward as credits for up to four years. The period commences on the day on or before which the return for the accounting period during which the credit could first have been claimed must be filed. As a practical matter, it will be prudent to claim credits as soon as possible in order to avoid carrying the cost of the input taxes. However, this rule is important for situations involving mistakes where credits were not claimed or other situations in which the actual credit amounts were not known at the time the original accounting period credits were claimed.

Vendors who are not registered under the system (such as small suppliers or persons providing exempt services, e.g., doctors) are required to collect and remit tax in respect of the taxable sale of real property. For example, a grocer that is a small supplier sells the building in which the store is operated in a taxable transaction. In these circumstances, the non-registrant will be obligated to file and remit tax in the same manner and in the same accounting periods as a registered vendor. For this purpose, the non-registrant's net tax amount will be the same as a registered vendor's net tax amount.

In certain special situations, a purchaser of real property will have an obligation to remit tax directly to the federal government and not pay it to a vendor. This will arise, for instance, where real property is acquired from a non-resident vendor. The purchaser will be required to file a return at the same time a return is required for the reporting period in which the sale occurred where the property was bought to be used exclusively in the course of the purchaser's commercial activities. In other cases, the return will be due on or before the last day of the month following the month in which tax became payable (i.e., was actually paid or the liability arose). For example, if the sale occured in March, the return would have to be filed no later than April 30.

Note that non-registered persons who are required to remit GST in a particular situation are required to do so within reporting periods established for non-registrants. A reporting period for this purpose is a calendar month.

Special rules apply to determine a vendor's net tax in respect of leased passenger vehicles. Restrictions are built in to mirror limitations on deductibility under the Income Tax Act.

Generally, input taxes on the lease payments will be creditable in the ordinary course. However, where the lease costs exceed the maximum deductible under the Income Tax Act (at present, $650 per month), then the input tax credits will be recaptured by the vendor at the end of the year.

A maximum input tax credit in respect of passenger vehicles is also imposed. Credits can only be claimed for taxes paid on the first $24,000 of capital cost of the vehicle. The recapture of these amounts is necessary at the end of a year because that is the only time that the income tax disallowance might be determined in many circumstances. The recapture will be made through an adjustment to the net tax amount of the vendor on the last return for the taxation year in question. Where the vendor is an annual filer or ceases to be registered in that year, then the adjustment will be made in the return for the first reporting period of the following year.

Input tax credit limitations are also imposed in respect of the cost of food, beverage and entertainment. Again, the limitations are intended to mirror restrictions on deductibility imposed by the Income Tax Act. In these circumstances, only 80% of the GST paid for these supplies will be available as a credit. In order to make accounting easier, a vendor will be allowed to claim full input tax credits during the course of a year and recapture the 20% balance at the end of the year. The 20% recapture will be added to the vendor's net tax amount at the end of the year. The object is to allow vendors to calculate their net input credits in respect of these supplies at the same time they can be calculated for income tax purposes.

b. Refunds

When input taxes exceed outputs, a vendor is entitled to the difference as a refund. Revenue Canada has the legal obligation to pay these refunds with all due dispatch after a return for the refund has been filed. Refunds will, however, only be available where the vendor has filed all returns required by the legislation up to that time. This last rule works as an incentive for vendors to file their returns on a timely basis.

The government will also have to pay interest on refunds until they are paid to an applicant. Interest will not start to accrue, though, until the later of 21 days from the day Revenue Canada received the return claiming the refund and the day on which all of the requirements respecting filing returns for previous periods have been satisfied. The interest will accrue until the day the refund is sent (i.e., mailed) to the applicant. For example, where a return claiming refund is filed for March and received by the

Minister on April 30 (the last day on which the return for March is due), interest charges will not begin until May 22. This rule will give taxpayers who file returns claiming refunds an incentive to either send the return by registered mail or by courier to establish the earliest possible date on which Revenue Canada has "received" the return. This will start the clock running in terms of the interest calculation. Each day lost means another day that an applicant has to finance the cost of an input credit.

Where GST remitted on account by a vendor (i.e., by way of instalment) exceeds the actual net tax amount that had to be remitted for the accounting period in question, a refund will be available. It can be obtained on the same terms as those noted above.

As an alternative to a refund, a vendor or even a purchaser can claim an adjustment to GST owing. Up to four years from the date the refund was recoverable will be available during which this adjustment can be claimed.

Where the price for supplies of goods or services, on which GST was originally determined, is reduced, an adjustment (or refund) will also be available. Where GST was not collected, but was remitted to the government, a refund or adjustment will be allowed and a refund can be passed on to the purchaser. Where GST was not collected or remitted, a credit will be available to the purchaser for the reduced purchase price. In these circumstances, a vendor must issue a credit note to the purchaser. The credit note can be deducted by the vendor when GST has been remitted. Similarly, the purchaser will have to add the credit note to its input taxes, in order to reduce them in light of the input tax recovered.

This procedure will not apply where a purchaser takes advantage of a prompt payment discount offered by the vendor. A credit note is not needed because there are no GST consequences in these situations as a result of a special rule designed to deal with early or late payment savings and charges. GST will apply to the full selling price of goods in spite of the fact that the purchaser enjoys a discount for prompt payment, or suffers additional charges for late payment (see Chapter III, "Computing GST," for details).

Where rebates are payable to individuals under the new residential housing rules, a vendor is allowed to credit the rebate to the purchaser at the time of the sale. The vendor can then claim the credit from net tax for the period. This allows builders to provide new housing credits to home buyers at the time of closing — and avoids any necessity of having the buyer finance the cost of the rebate until it can be refunded through the system.

c. Quick Accounting Method

The GST was made liveable for hundreds of thousands of small businesses on May 31, 1990, when Revenue Minister Otto Jelinek announced a new accounting method for a significant portion of vendors that will be subject to the tax. This method will allow vendors to multiply total sales for a period by the applicable percentage for the business and remit the amount to the government. This will remove the need to keep track of GST inputs as well as GST collected on sales for reporting purposes.

In theory, the GST will be an easy tax to administer. As noted earlier, vendors will pay tax on everything they buy, collect tax on everything they sell and send the net difference between the two amounts to the government.

Simple? Unfortunately not.

Businesses pay for hundreds or thousands of goods and services annually to keep operations afloat, from stationery to rent, electricity and inventories. GST will be paid on all of those supplies and documentation will have to be kept to substantiate claims for input tax credits.

A big problem with documentation is that no special GST "invoice" rule (discussed in more detail later in this chapter) has been established. Thus, vendors will be forced to keep all types of documents, from invoices to way bills, contracts and cash register receipts to evidence that the tax has been paid on purchases.

While much of the documentation that a vendor would have to keep for income tax purposes will be sufficient for GST, a lot won't. For example, many businesses don't rely on invoices issued by a supplier but rather use a system of cancelled cheques to keep track of purchases. Under GST, a cancelled cheque will probably not be enough.

On the other end, businesses sell under a variety of circumstances that can make keeping track of GST collected difficult. Discounts, sales, volume purchases and warranty relief all affect the amount of GST that must be collected, remitted and kept track of. While net sales figures can be readily determined, they may not necessarily reflect the GST base. Even cash registers that can accommodate GST as an extra charge cannot keep track of all adjustments needed to determine final liabilities.

Small businesses were going to have the most problems. Barbers, taxi drivers and carpenters for the most part simply do not have accounting systems sophisticated enough to deal with GST compliance. Grocers were going to be particularly hard hit because they would have to segregate between taxable sales and their zero-rated food sales (though they still have to know the breakdown for pricing purposes).

The new accounting package (the Quick Method) announced by the Minister will solve those problems for small business. With it, vendors will not have to keep a paper trail of GST paid on purchases or total amounts collected on sales. The method is available at a vendor's choice and can either be chosen or dropped from year to year.

GST remitted to the government will be based on a percentage of sales. Where sales of basic groceries (zero-rated) are over 50%, vendors will remit 1% of their total sales as a notional net GST liability. Where grocery sales are between 25% and 50%, the net liability factor will be 1.75%. These two factors will apply to grocery and convenience stores, greengrocers, butchers, bakeries and other similar businesses with sales of basic groceries that exceed these limits.

In all other cases, the net liability factor will be either 3% or 5%, depending on the category of small business the vendor is in. Manufacturers and service vendors, such as sawmills, bodyshops, electricians, barbers and hairstylists, construction contractors and repair shops, will fall within the 5% category. Retailers and wholesalers, such as clothing and shoe stores, hardware stores and vendors selling less than 25% basic groceries will attract the 3% category. Note that this method will not be available to legal, accounting and financial accounting businesses.

The new method will be available for vendors with annual sales of up to $200,000. Grocery and convenience stores will be able to use the Quick Method where their sales do not exceed $500,000.

In practical terms, the Quick Method will be useful where full compliance is prohibitive both in terms of time and cost. Since the net liability factors were based on averaged statistical evidence, some businesses may even find that they are paying less GST under the Quick Method than they otherwise would.

In many cases, it will be best to keep track of inputs and outputs for the first year and compare the net tax liability payable to the percentage liability under this method. If the differences between the two are not significant and compliance costs can be saved, the Quick Method will be the smart choice every time for those that can use it.

d. Streamlined Accounting Method

A separate accounting method will be available for registrants of a prescribed class (to be identified by regulation). The object of this method is to simplify compliance requirements for vendors selling both taxable and zero-rated supplies (the largest category being food).

The simplified accounting method allows vendors to use estimates of GST outputs, rather than actual figures. This will limit their need to track actual sales of taxable supplies in comparison to sales of zero-rated supplies.

Without some method of estimating outputs in these situations, many taxpayers would be faced with impossible tasks of tracking actual sales. While this is possible for vendors with sophisticated point-of-sale equipment, smaller operations (particularly manually based ones) would find the process unbearable. The actual mechanics of estimating GST outputs (which are prescribed by regulation) could also be problematical in some instances. Two methods were suggested by the August 9, 1989, proposals.

The first method is based on regular selling prices of taxable goods, which are then used to determine estimated GST outputs. Problems can occur, however, when prices are marked down or discounted at sale. This will result in the payment of higher outputs than would actually be required. Furthermore, vendors using this method will have to remit GST in respect of their inventories on hand at the time use of the method begins, based on their regular selling price at that time. For the first year of the system, GST outputs can be remitted on a quarterly basis (resulting in the potential for pre-payment of GST in some situations). Credits will be available when the vendor drops out of the streamlined accounting election.

The second method is based on using a prescribed (fixed by regulation) mark-up of zero-rated basic groceries. The value of marked-up grocery inventories will be deducted from total sales for the period to arrive at a GST output estimate. The problem with this method is that it can result in either an overstatement or understatement of zero-rated sales for the period (though upper and lower limit restrictions will be imposed to reduce this effect). If groceries are sold at lower than average mark-up, it will result in lower GST outputs. Conversely, where sales are higher than average mark-up, then higher GST outputs can result. This will provide vendors with an incentive to make significant zero-rated inventory purchases at the end of a period in order to obtain advantages in relation to the GST output estimate, given the effect of averaging.

Vendors entitled to choose these accounting methods must do so by election. The election will be available to registrants with annual sales less than $2 million. However, until 1993 these methods will be available to businesses with sales between $2 million and $6 million. Elections will have to be filed with Revenue Canada on or before the last day for filing the vendor's return for the accounting period in which the election is to become effective. The form must also identify the first day of the accounting period in which the election is effective. For applicants filing annually, the election can be made by the first day of the second fiscal quarter in the year in which the election is to take effect.

Elections will automatically expire on the earlier of the day the applicant's reporting period in which the business ceases to qualify as a prescribed retail establishment, or the last day of the reporting period in which a revocation of the election is filed with Revenue Canada.

Once an election expires, a vendor will have to determine net tax in accordance with the prescribed manner. This is designed to allow adjustments required to accommodate the transition between the streamlined system and the normal rules.

5. Instalments

Vendors with total annual taxable sales of less than $500,000 in the immediately preceding fiscal year must pay the GST by instalments. Government estimates indicate that this category will represent more than one million registrants (the majority of businesses expected to register under the new system).

Instalments will have to be made quarterly, on or before the last day of each fiscal quarter. The payments will be equal to one-quarter of the vendor's "instalment base" for the reporting period (i.e., annual) in question.

A vendor's instalment base for an annual reporting period will be the lesser of two amounts (note that special transitional measures apply for GST implementation and are discussed below):

- The vendor's net tax for the period (see "Remitting GST," earlier in the chapter for more details), and

- The vendor's net tax for all reporting periods ending in the 12- month period that immediately precedes the particular reporting period. For example, if a vendor's net tax for 1992 was $16,000 and its net tax for 1993 was $18,000, the instalment base would be $16,000, resulting in quarterly instalment liabilities of $4,000 each. If the vendor's net tax for 1993 was $12,000, the instalment base would be $12,000, resulting in quarterly instalment liabilities of $3,000 each.

One practical difficulty relates to determining the current year's net tax. To solve the problem, vendors will be allowed to estimate annual sales. Penalties and interest will be charged when estimates turn out to be too low, resulting in an understated instalment base.

When a vendor no longer qualifies for annual reporting at any time (i.e., when sales exceed the $500,000 annual threshold), a short period will be created on the transition. In these situations, the vendor can gross up its net tax amount for the short period to an equivalent amount for the 12-month period in order to determine the instalment base for that short period.

A minimum instalment base is set at $1,000. When a vendor's base is less than $1,000 for any period, the base will be deemed to be nil. The vendor will still have to file annual returns, however, with remittance of GST outputs under the $1,000. Where a vendor's net tax for a period is negative (i.e., when a refund is entitled), it will be assumed to be nil for instalment base calculations.

A preferential transitional rule has been established for 1991. For this year, a vendor's instalment base will be equal to the lesser of two amounts:

- 75% of the vendor's net tax for the period, and
- A prescribed percentage (set by regulation) of the total consideration for supplies made by the vendor in the 1991 fiscal period, either pro-rated or grossed up to reflect a 365-day year. This will accommodate vendors that do not have calendar-year fiscal periods.

6. Reporting GST

All registrants are obligated to file returns for each reporting period. Reporting periods (discussed below) are, with some exceptions, monthly, quarterly and annually, depending on sales volumes.

Returns must be filed within one month from the end of a particular reporting period. For example, if a reporting period ends in March, the return must be filed by April 30. An exception is available for registrants who file annually. They are not required to file returns until after three months from the end of their fiscal year.

Non-registrants are also obligated to file returns with Revenue Canada when they have provided taxable supplies in Canada during a reporting period (which is deemed to be a calendar month for non-registrants). The returns must be filed no later than one month after the end of the particular calendar month in which the taxable supplies were made.

A special rule has been established for returns by non-residents that sell admissions (which are taxable) to performances, exhibits, seminars or any other activities or events of a similar nature. They will initially be subject to the ordinary reporting requirements for non-residents. However, if they are leaving Canada before the time for filing a return has expired (which will often be the case), they will be required to file a return before they leave.

In some cases, it will be more advantageous for different branches or divisions of the same organization (such as a corporation) to file separate returns for each reporting period. In these situations, the registrant will be able to apply to Revenue Canada for authorization to have the branches or divisions file separately.

As long as Revenue Canada is satisfied that the branches or divisions have separate accounting systems and are easily identifiable by virtue of their location or activities, they will be allowed to file separate returns. This authorization can be revoked, however, when Revenue Canada believes that it is no longer necessary, or the requirements necessary to the authorization are no longer being satisfied. Revenue Canada will provide written notice of the revocation, along with an effective date.

As noted above, a registrant's reporting period will determine both the time returns must be filed and GST outputs remitted. In general terms, registrants will have a single fiscal year as a basic reporting period. For quarterly and monthly filers, the year is broken into smaller reporting periods (i.e., monthly and quarterly).

Registrants will be given the option to choose the same reporting period as they have for income tax purposes. This will be advantageous in practical terms, where accounting functions for both filings can take place at the same time.

Individuals or trusts that have more than one fiscal period for income tax purposes will be allowed to select any of those periods for GST purposes. Alternatively, they can choose a calendar year as a GST reporting period.

Fiscal periods relate to reporting periods. That is, once a registrant's fiscal period is determined, it will fix a reporting period that coincides. If a person's fiscal year is a calendar year, their fiscal quarter and fiscal month will correspondingly be a calendar quarter (January-March; April-June; July-September; October-December) and calendar months respectively. If a person's fiscal year is not a calendar year, separate rules will apply to determine their fiscal quarter and fiscal months.

There cannot be more than four fiscal quarters in the year, with the first beginning on the first day of the fiscal year and the last quarter ending on the last day of the fiscal period. The fiscal quarters cannot be longer than 114 days.

Similarly, fiscal months cannot be longer than 35 days each and the first and last fiscal months cannot be shorter than 28 days. The first fiscal month in each fiscal quarter must begin on the first day of the fiscal quarter and the last fiscal month must end on the last day of that quarter.

Registrants can also elect to have GST fiscal years that are different from their taxation years for income tax purposes. In some cases, this will be advisable in order to maximize cash flows.

This election will, however, only allow a taxpayer to choose the calendar year as a fiscal year for GST purposes. Thus, a different year for GST purposes will only be available where the person's income tax year is different from the calendar year.

As noted above, a person can elect to have a GST fiscal year that is the same as their income taxation year. The elections will be effective on the first day of the fiscal period in question and must be filed on a prescribed form within one month from the effective date. Elections will be binding for at least one year and may thereafter be revoked by the registrant.

A reporting period will be based on a registrant's threshold for a period. A threshold is basically the amount of taxable sales made in a period.

A threshold amount for a fiscal year or a fiscal quarter is identified in relation to the registrant's taxable sales or supply (including all zero-rated sales) made in the preceding year or quarter. For example, a manufacturer's 1992 threshold amount for these purposes would be based on its sales in fiscal 1991.

Threshold amounts are determined by formula. The threshold amount for a fiscal year is based on all taxable supplies made in the immediately preceding fiscal year. For this purpose, taxable supplies exclude financial services and capital real property dispositions.

This threshold will include taxable supplies (with zero-rated sales) made by all associated persons (in that year that were also associated in the year) and will be pro-rated where the preceding fiscal year was less than 12 months in length. New corporations formed by way of amalgamation or wind-up are to include the taxable supplies made by the predecessors.

Threshold amounts for a fiscal quarter will be based on all taxable supplies made during all preceding fiscal quarters in the fiscal year in question. Again, the taxable supplies of associated persons are counted (with zero-rated sales) and financial services or capital real property sales are excluded.

The threshold mechanism allows for the timely and efficient movement of registrants between the different reporting periods based on sales volume. Three actual thresholds are set:

- If a registrant's threshold for a preceding year is less than $500,000, it can elect to file on a fiscal year basis. Thus, returns need not be filed until three months after the end of that year, but quarterly instalments have to be made relative to the registrant's instalment base.
- If a registrant's threshold for a fiscal year or fiscal quarter exceeds $6 million, monthly filing will be required.
- In all other circumstances (i.e., where threshold sales are between $500,000 and $6 million), registrants will be allowed to file returns on a quarterly basis.

Sales volumes less than $500,000 and more than $6 million for a fiscal year are relatively easy to determine. It will be a bit trickier to follow sales of $6 million for fiscal quarters.

Basically, all of the fiscal quarters preceding the fiscal quarter of the moment (that is the subject of a return) are to be added together to determine whether sales have exceeded the $6 million threshold.

For example, assume that sales for the first three fiscal quarters of 1992 are $7.5 million. An obligation to file monthly would arise in the fourth quarter of 1992. Further, monthly filing would have to start for the first month of that quarter.

Conversely, if sales for 1991 remained at $5 million and sales for the first three quarters of 1992 were at $5.9 million, an obligation to file monthly would not arise in the fourth quarter of 1992. Rather, assuming sales caused the registrant to go over the $6-million limit in 1992, an obligation to file monthly would begin in the first quarter of 1993 (i.e., because the threshold would have been exceeded in the previous fiscal "year" of the registrant).

Registrants reporting quarterly or annually can elect to file monthly. This will be beneficial to registrants who are in a consistent position to obtain refunds (i.e., zero-rated food sellers or export sales vendors). They should recover GST inputs as soon as possible in order to reduce financing costs.

Elections, when chosen, will be effective for persons already registered on the first day of a fiscal year (so the change cannot be made during mid-year). For new registrants, the election can be made effective the first day the applicant becomes registered (which effectively is its first day of its first fiscal year).

There is one exception to the rule that elections are effective on the first day of a registrant's fiscal year. When sales thresholds exceed the $500,000 limit for a registrant's second or third fiscal quarters (requiring quarterly filing beginning in the fourth fiscal quarter), the registrant can elect to make monthly filing.

These elections will be effective until the registrants choose to revert to either quarterly or annual filing (which may be advantageous when they reach a stage of remitting GST). The reverting elections can be made when threshold sales for those filing options have not been exceeded (ie., sales for annual filers remain less than $500,000 and sales for quarterly filers are less than $6 million).

First-time registrants establish reporting periods at the time they become registered. The initial reporting period will begin on the first day of the calendar month and finish on the day immediately preceding the effective registration date. The second reporting period will be the period spanning the effective registration date and ending at the end of the calendar month in question.

For example, if a corporation registers on January 15, the first reporting period would cover January 1 to January 14. The second reporting period would cover January 15 to January 31. Monthly, quarterly or annual reporting periods would then follow, as the case may be.

In most situations, there would be no need to file a return for the first reporting period, because there would be no taxable sales during that time. Returns would have to be filed if taxable sales did, however, occur in that period.

When a person ceases to be registered under GST, a separate reporting period will be established for the period ending on the day before the effective date of revocation. A return will be required within one month of that time, or three months if the registrant was an annual filer.

7. Record Keeping

All persons who carry on a business or commercial activity that is required to file GST returns (whether registrants or non-registrants), as well as anyone who claims refunds or rebates under the transitional provisions, are required to keep records for GST purposes. These records must contain sufficient information to determine all rebates or refunds (also called liabilities, obligations or entitlements) under GST.

The records must be kept in Canada, although Revenue Canada can grant permission to keep records outside the country (i.e., such as in a central computer bank in the United States).

As a general rule, records have to be kept for six years, similar to the income tax system. Other periods can be prescribed by regulation and Revenue Canada has the authority to require or permit other periods.

When the records relate to the application of the transitional provisions in a proceeding (i.e., a court challenge of entitlement), the records have to be retained until the proceeding is completed (which in some cases can take longer than six years).

Revenue Canada is entitled to inspect these records at reasonable times and can enter premises or a place of business to do so. Persons on those premises have an obligation to provide reasonable assistance and answer all proper questions. Revenue Canada can enter dwelling-houses only by permission or under a search warrant. Revenue Canada has the power to require any person to supply information or documents for the purposes of administering or enforcing the GST system. This might include, for example, a consumer who is required to provide a sales receipt.

When documents are seized, inspected, or otherwise examined or provided, Revenue Canada has the right to make copies of the document. Certified copies are to be treated as originals for GST purposes. The public has an obligation not to hinder, molest or interfere with Revenue Canada officials who are authorized to inspect, seize or examine documents.

Revenue Canada can also require non-residents and residents to provide access to records maintained outside Canada that are relevant to the transitional provisions. If there is a failure to comply, then the foreign-based information will not be admissible as evidence in any civil proceeding regarding those provisions.

Solicitor-client privilege may be claimed regarding documents or records in the possession of a lawyer. When the claim is mailed, the information will be packaged and sealed pending a determination of the privilege.

A special rule has been established for corporations resident in Canada which carry on business in Canada and enter into transactions with non-residents related to the corporation in the taxation year. They must file an information return with Revenue Canada in the proscribed form within six months from the end of the year in which the transactions took place.

8. Input Tax Credits

Input taxes are the equivalent of cash to vendors, as well as other registrants under the system, and should be treated accordingly. They represent the GST that a registrant has paid on obtaining the goods and services necessary to commercial operations and activities. For taxable and zero-rated registrants, the input taxes are completely recoverable, either as an offset against GST remittances and (ultimately) instalments, or as a direct refund, when applied for.

The general rule states that taxes paid or payable by a registrant for the acquisition of a supply of goods or services that are acquired for consumption, use or supply in the course of the registrant's commercial activities can be claimed as a credit. The claim can be made in the reporting period during which the tax either was paid or became payable, whichever is earlier.

When there is an invoice for a supply, the date on the invoice will be considered to be the date the GST became payable for the purpose of claiming input credits in a period.

This rule applies to registrants making taxable and zero-rated sales. A separate rule has been established for exempt sales. Registrants making exempt sales cannot, as a rule, recover GST inputs. However, nothing prevents a registrant that makes both taxable (or zero-rated) sales and exempt sales from recovering inputs incurred in relation to the taxable sales.

A special rule has been established to apportion inputs for partial use between taxable sales and exempt or personal uses. Thus, if a lathe is used 35% of the time to make cabinets that are sold in taxable transactions and 65% to make personal use furniture, only 35% of the GST paid on the acquisition of the lathe can be claimed as an input credit.

When a supply is used "exclusively" in taxable activities, the entire GST input will be creditable. For this purpose, the term "exclusively" is defined to mean 90%.

It will be up to a registrant to make this allocation based on a factual assessment of the circumstances of use. Note that Revenue Canada can challenge an allocation and, if successful, can impose interest and penalties for inputs incorrectly credited.

Although most businesses will be able to recover GST inputs during operations, providing Revenue Canada with the documentation necessary to do so could prove onerous. If the process is not carefully managed, a relatively straightforward procedure could become a real burden and result in lost revenues.

Vendors will have an obligation to show purchasers that GST liabilities have been satisfied in one of two ways:

- Receipts issued by a vendor will have to show the actual

amount of GST paid on the taxable supply of goods and services, or

- Invoices or cash register receipts will have to indicate that the prices charged for the taxable goods and services already include GST.

However, receipts do not have to be issued in all circumstances. Contracts, purchase orders or other documents that identify GST liability will be acceptable. These documents will be necessary to support input tax credit claims. Without them, tax will not be recoverable.

As a general rule, however, registrants have an obligation to obtain sufficient evidence in a form and containing information (including any information that is required by regulation) that will enable Revenue Canada to determine the amount of inputs.

The problem with this approach is that no standardized system of documentation will be established to track input tax. In many countries, where similar multi-stage consumption taxes have been adopted (such as VAT in the United Kingdom), a special "tax invoicing" system was implemented as a means of creating one document to act as a single source of input tax identification. The federal government has chosen not to adopt this practice. Rather, in order to support claims for input tax credits, taxpayers will be obligated to keep any contracts, invoices or receipts that have been issued by suppliers as proof of the tax paid.

Although this might not seem particularly difficult, transactions often involve a multitude of documents to evidence a sale, as opposed to a simple invoice. A single transaction could include tenders, contracts, work orders and bills of sale or lading in addition to conventional sales receipts.

It is far from clear whether some or all of those documents would be necessary to substantiate input credit claims. It is clear, however, that each case will be different, resulting in millions of dissimilar documents that will have to be scrutinized by Revenue Canada auditors. Real problems will occur when taxpayers and the government disagree on the required documentation, resulting in denied input credit claims.

In the fall of 1989, the issue was canvassed at a conference (held in Canada) by Graham Holland, who completed his 25 years with the New Zealand Inland Revenue Department by leading the team that implemented that country's goods and services tax. After reviewing the Canadian proposals, he questioned the wisdom of allowing free reign on the form and type of documents that might substantiate input credit claims. In his view, a single tax invoice would simplify administering input claims and reduce opportunities for fraud that will exist when several documents from the same transaction can be used for multiple refunds. He further suggested that concerns expressed by the Department of Finance over creating additional paperwork could be overcome by simply having one document that would otherwise exist in a transaction stamped as a tax invoice.

As noted later (see "Invoicing" later in this chapter), different information will be required depending on the amount of a particular sale. A vendor will have to supply this information with sales documentation and purchasers can demand it when not supplied.

The different levels are as follows:

- For sales under $30, a vendor's sales documents must include its name and any information that proves GST was paid or became payable.
- For sales between $30 and $150, in addition to the information above, the documents must include the actual GST liability, or a statement that GST was included in the price, along with the vendor's GST registration number.
- Finally, for sales over $150, the information required on documents must also include the buyer's name (or trading name) or the name of its agent or representative. Further, the document has to identify the terms of sale and must describe the supply that has been made.

Invoices will not be required to prove some types of input claims. These include items bought from vending machines and reasonable payments made to employees to reimburse meal, automobile and other incidental expenses incurred for business trips in Canada.

Revenue Canada will also be free to exempt registrants from the need to have invoices in cases where it would be impractical for vendors to issue them or if there are other documents that can provide evidence that tax has been paid or is payable.

In light of these considerations, registrants may choose to initiate their own internal tax-invoicing system that will standardize documentation within their particular organizations. This practice would probably reduce the potential for disputes on the issue with Revenue Canada auditors.

Revenue Canada will have the administrative discretion to exempt registrants from these general documentation requirements if it is satisfied that claims are clearly supported by records or other information readily available.

Similar to the Income Tax Act, input credits will be available only to the extent that they are reasonable in the circumstances, having regard to a registrant's commercial operations. Both the nature and the extent of the supply must be reasonable within this context. For greater certainty, a number of specific limitations have been established to deny the recovery of GST inputs. These include GST paid for:

- Club memberships, where the main purpose of the club is to provide sporting, dining or recreational facilities.
- Goods or services acquired by a registrant exclusively ("exclusively" is defined as more than 90%) for the personal use, enjoyment or consumption of either an officer, employee or related individual of the registrant. Note that this limitation will not apply if the supply was made by the registrant to the officer or employee at a price that represents its fair market value (if the supply was made within four years from the reporting period in which it was acquired by the registrant). The limitation will also not apply if the benefit would not

represent a taxable benefit for income tax purposes had it been provided free of charge.

- Property supplied under a lease, licence or similar arrangement for the personal enjoyment, use or consumption by the registrant (if an individual) or a related individual. Alternatively, the property is supplied to an individual that is (or is related to) an employee, officer, shareholder or beneficiary (i.e., such as a trust beneficiary) of the registrant. This limitation will not apply if the property was supplied at its fair market value price, as long as payment was made before the end of the reporting period in which the supply was made. This limitation can cause problems for monthly fliers who provide a vacation condominium for employees at the end of a month for a period that straddles the following reporting period of the employer. Payment would have to be made in the middle of the employee's vacation in order that the employer did not lose entitlement to inputs for that period.
- Passenger vehicles will be subject to limitations that mirror those in the Income Tax Act. Thus, if the capital cost of a vehicle exceeds certain limits, GST paid on the cost of the vehicle over and above those limits will not be recoverable as an input credit (see "Remitting GST," discussed earlier in this chapter for more details).

As stated earlier ("Remitting GST"), input credits claimed in one reporting period cannot be claimed in any subsequent reporting period. Further, registrants will have four years in which to claim credits. The four-year period begins on the day on or before which the return for the particular reporting period was required to be filed. In this regard, it is very important to note that it is not the date the return was actually filed for the period, but the date the return was required to be filed. Thus, registrants will have to be careful that they do not start clocks running too soon. Similarly, if returns for a particular period are filed late, the period will begin before that date, on the day filing should have occurred. Again, this could cause problems in cases where the four-year period expires prior to the time inputs are claimed.

A four-year period was chosen because of a similar period available under the federal sales tax system. It will be particularly useful in situations where input liabilities are adjusted subsequent to acquisitions, or where they are changed as a result of litigation.

Input taxes will also be limited for vendors who supply a residential complex on a tax-exempt basis. Once the supply has been made, the vendor will be prohibited from claiming GST inputs in relation to that supply.

A planning point to keep in mind: Taxable parties should attempt, whenever possible, to buy from taxable vendors. Buying exempt services or goods, or buying from small suppliers that have not registered, means that GST inputs of those vendors are probably part of the purchase price. However, when a purchase is not taxable, input credits cannot be claimed. That means the hidden GST costs will not be recovered. Many small suppliers will choose to be registered and taxable for this reason.

9. Computing GST: How Much to Pay and Collect

As a general rule, GST will be based on the value of "consideration" for a taxable supply. The term "consideration" is a legal concept that embraces anything that someone might pay for goods or services. This will include money or payments in kind, as well as any other benefits (both tangible and intangible) that might be received, used or enjoyed by a vendor or anyone else who benefits as a result of the sale (such as a relative).

To recap: The amount paid for the taxable supply (with some adjustments discussed below) will be the base for GST purposes.

Keep in mind that parties to an agreement or arrangement (which includes retail sales) can negotiate the price of a taxable supply to either include, or exclude taxes, such as the GST. When a tax-included price is negotiated, the gross selling price is not the

GST base. Rather, the GST base is equal to the gross selling price, minus the GST component. Identifying the GST component of a tax-included selling price is easily done using a simple formula. The price is multiplied by 7/107ths. Alternatively, the net price of the tax-included supply, excluding GST, is determined by multiplying the gross price by 100/107ths. For example, if the tax-included selling price of a jacket is $100, the GST component is $100 x 7/107 = $6.54 and the net selling price of the jacket is $93.46.

Problems can arise when a selling price is negotiated but it has not been stated whether the price includes or excludes GST. A purchaser would want to argue that the price is inclusive. In that way, taxable purchasers can recover the GST component of the price as an input credit and the net selling price is the purchaser's full cost. A vendor, on the other hand, would argue that the price is exclusive of GST. In this way, the gross price represents the full return that the vendor experiences on the sale.

When the price does not refer to GST and matters are left as they are, Revenue Canada will probably insist that the full price represents the consideration on which GST is to be calculated and will require the vendor to remit that amount. The vendor will then be forced to look to the purchaser for the GST component and will have a right to sue for that amount as if it were a debt.

At that point, the purchaser has to either pay the GST or defend the action on the basis that the price was tax inclusive. As a practical matter, it would be best to avoid this issue by ensuring that the matter of GST is addressed in all taxable transactions.

Generally, the value of consideration will be easy to determine because actual cash changes hands. However, where property, rather than cash, is used as consideration (such as barter or exchange transactions) the fair market value of that property at the time of the taxable supply will be the consideration on which GST is calculated.

Note that in barter transactions, the parties will have to come up with actual cash to pay GST liabilities on the exchanged goods or services. Note also that Revenue Canada can challenge the fair market value of the property or service chosen by the parties, if it is considered either too high or low. In these circumstances, it will be prudent for parties to obtain independent valuations to substantiate their claims.

Revenue Canada is allowed to reasonably apportion the consideration paid for a supply in situations where amounts paid for several supplies and/or for other obligations have been unreasonably apportioned. The object of this rule is to ensure that the full GST liability is properly identified where consideration relates to both taxable and non-taxable transactions.

Some taxes will be included in the GST base, while others will be excluded. The taxes included are:

- Taxes, duties or fees (other than prescribed amounts) that are imposed on the supplier or recipient of the supply under a federal or provincial statute. For example, this would include customs and excise duties and air transportation tax or excise taxes imposed by the Excise Tax Act.
- Provincial sales taxes that do not fall within prescribed categories established by the regulations. It is proposed that sales taxes in excess of 12% will be part of the GST base.

The excluded taxes are:

- GST liabilities in relation to the supply (necessary to avoid double taxation).
- It is proposed that provincial sales taxes imposed at rates that are less than 13% be excluded.

An avoidance provision will limit the ability of taxpayers to circumvent the GST system by transferring property or services for no consideration or less than fair-market-value consideration. The transfers must be made in non-arm's-length transactions to persons who are not registrants or who will use the supply in the course of making an exempt supply. In these situations, Revenue Canada will be authorized to deem the transfer to have taken place at fair market value. A similar rule applies when a non-registrant sells used goods to a registrant in a non-arm's-length transaction.

This rule will not apply when the supply is made between two non-arm's-length parties and the recipient is registered under GST. However, the supply must be used by the recipient exclusively in the course of a commercial enterprise.

A special election is provided for taxable supplies made between closely related corporations to treat the transactions as being zero-rated (i.e., no GST is payable on the supply, but the vendors are entitled to recover input taxes). To be effective, the election must be filed jointly by the participating corporations. This rule is necessary in order not to penalize related groups of companies for inter-group sales (i.e., by forcing GST remittances and extra cash flow burdens) in comparison to divisionalized single corporations that would not experience GST charges on inter-departmental transfers. Zero-rating will not be available under this rule for sales of real property or any supply that is not acquired exclusively for use in a commercial enterprise.

Corporations must be closely related for the purpose of this election when they are resident in Canada and there is a degree of common ownership of at least 90% between the groups. Thus, parent and subsidiaries that are more than 90% owned will be related, as will sister corporations that are each more than 90% owned by the same controlling shareholder(s).

Coupons presented by purchasers will reduce the price on which GST is calculated. For example, if a 75¢ coupon for mouthwash reduces the cost to a consumer from $4.00 to $3.25, GST will be 7% of the reduced price, i.e., 26¢.

Though products subject to coupons are sold by one vendor (such as a retailer), the coupons are often offered as incentives by another registrant, such as the manufacturer. Normally, the vendor will seek reimbursement from the registrant for all coupons honoured. Rules have been established to ensure that the reimbursement is not subject to GST and does not result in any limits on either party's ability to claim input credits.

With regard to gift certificates, a taxable supply will not be considered to have occurred at the time the certificate is issued. Rather, GST will arise when the certificate is used for a purchase. The interesting point is whether gift certificates can be used to pay GST liabilities of purchasers. For example, can a $20 purchase, plus $1.40 GST, be paid with a $50 gift certificate?

Nothing in the legislation seems to prevent this practice. Revenue Canada should be happy as long as the proper remittance is made in the circumstances. It will therefore be up to individual vendors to set business policies in this regard.

GST liabilities are always to be determined in Canadian dollar equivalents. When the price of a taxable supply is expressed in foreign currency, GST liability will be determined with reference to the Canadian dollar equivalent, after converting the foreign currency. The effective conversion rate will be the one posted on the day the consideration is paid or becomes payable.

Note that Revenue Canada will have the discretion to accept other methods of determining Canadian dollar equivalents in these situations. The overriding consideration is that the method chosen be reasonable in the circumstances and that it is followed consistently by the business in question.

Special rules are established for certain industries. For coin-operated vending machines (or any other coin-operated devices), purchasers will be considered to have paid GST at the time the purchase is made (i.e., vending machines will offer a tax included price).

GST will be considered to have become collectible when the cash is removed from the machines, at which time the supply will be deemed to have been made. Thus, although purchasers will be considered to have incurred input taxes at the time a purchase was made, vendors will be considered to have made a sale only at the time funds were removed from a machine.

Determining GST for tour packages can be challenging. As a general proposition, only some parts of a tour package will be subject to tax. Other parts will be excluded on the basis that they are incurred outside the country.

Tour operators selling packages are obligated to pro-rate costs between taxable and non-taxable portions of supplies provided. The pro-ration has to be completed on the basis of the relative value of each service.

Normally, this pro-ration will have to be done only once — at the time the package is originally costed out. However, an obligation to redetermine the GST portion of the cost will exist when the factors on which the original pro-ration was based change.

When tour operators act as wholesalers, selling packages to retailers, the price charged to a consumer will be subject to the same GST pro-ration formula used by the retailer on acquisition of the package from the wholesaler. Thus, if a retailer pays GST on 60% of the cost of the package to the wholesaler, GST will be payable on 60% of the cost of the package to a consumer.

As a general rule, charitable and political donations are not subject to GST. GST will not be payable even when the payments made include consideration for the donation and for the receipt of a taxable supply, such as dinner at a fund-raising event. The catch is that the donation must be one that would qualify as a charitable donation or political contribution for income tax purposes.

10. Invoicing: What to Show

Vendors selling taxable goods and services will be able to choose between showing GST as an extra amount on invoices or as an amount included in the selling price. A pair of shoes can either be billed at $107 tax included, or at $100, plus GST.

It's up to each vendor to decide what to do. Either way, vendors will have to indicate that GST was part of the selling price.

The psychology of establishing selling prices has been clear for centuries. Vendors try to make the price "seem" as low as possible. Much has been written on products (and businesses) that have lived or died on the nuance between sale prices of $9.99 and $10.00. It is likely that many retailers will try to present prices that exclude tax, i.e., $100 plus tax.

As discussed earlier ("Input Tax Credits"), vendors have a responsibility to show, in documented form, that GST liabilities have been satisfied in one of two ways:

- Either receipts issued by a vendor must show the actual amount of GST paid on the taxable supply of goods and services, or
- Invoices or cash register receipts will have to indicate that the prices charged for the taxable goods and services already include GST.

When receipts are not issued, contracts, purchase orders or other documents that identify GST liability will be acceptable. These documents will be necessary to support input tax credit claims. Without them, the tax will not be recoverable. As a result, purchasers will put enormous pressure on vendors to issue some form of documentation detailing GST. Many businesses that didn't use receipts much before GST will find their commercial practices have to change. These practices can be found at all trade levels, including retail and wholesale but particularly at the manufacturing level.

Depending on the value of goods or services supplied, vendors have an obligation to provide certain information in addition to price. This information is necessary for purchasers to substantiate their input credit claims. Three levels have been established:

- For sales under $30, the vendor has to provide documents that include its name and any information that is capable of proving that GST was paid or became payable.
- For sales between $30 and $150, the documents must also

show the actual GST liability, or a statement that GST was included in the price, along with the vendor's GST registration number.

- For sales over $150, the information required above must be included, as well as the buyer's name (or trading name) or the name of its agent or representative. The document must identify the terms of sale, such as whether it was on cash or credit, whether discounts are available for prompt payment or the time over which payments must be made. Finally, the goods or services supplied must be described.

Purchasers have the right to require vendors to issue documents detailing this information.

11. Used Goods

Used goods sold between non-registrants (i.e., consumers) will not be subject to GST. That is, the seller won't have to charge tax on the sale and neither the seller nor purchaser will be able to recover GST inputs, if any, that may be inherent in the purchase price of the used goods.

Used goods are broken into two categories:

- Used tangible personal property, and
- Specified tangible personal property.

The distinction between the two is simple; one refers to appreciating used goods and the other covers all other used goods (the normal kind that usually depreciate).

Specified tangible personal property is defined to reflect the listed personal property definition in the Income Tax Act. It generally includes works of art, jewellery, rare books, stamps and coins. Used tangible personal property refers to all other types of used goods.

The difference between the two types of property for GST purposes lies in the notional input tax credits (discussed below) that are available in respect of their purchase by different categories of purchasers.

As a general rule, when used goods are sold by registrants, the sale will be subject to GST in the ordinary course. Alternatively, when used goods are acquired by a registrant from a non-registrant, the sale will not be subject to GST.

To avoid double taxation, however, special rules are needed to provide registrants who buy used goods from non-registrants with credit for the GST that is notionally inherent in the used goods (i.e., the tax that was paid by the vendor on the original purchase of the used goods).

Thus, the legislation provides that registrants who buy used goods from non-registrants are entitled to a notional input tax credit on the purchase. These credits will be recaptured where the registrant subsequently sells the goods on a zero-rated basis (i.e., as in exports, discussed in more detail later on).

This credit will be available when the goods were purchased from non-registrants or registrants that did not employ the used goods in a commercial enterprise. Furthermore, the registrant has to acquire the used goods for use, consumption or supply in the course of its commercial activities.

The notional input credit will be determined on the basis of a simple calculation. Registrants will be entitled to claim an input credit equal to the purchase price multiplied by 7/107ths. For example, assume that a re-sale clothing shop buys dresses from a customer for $200. It would be allowed a notional input credit equal to $200 x 7/107 = $13.08.

The determination of notional input credits on used goods sales will, for transitional purposes, be subject to different rules for sales occurring before 1994 and those occurring after 1993.

For sales occurring after 1993, the notional credit will be available to any registrant that buys used goods from non-registrants. Alternatively, for sales taking place before 1994, the notional input credit will be available only for registrants who buy them for subsequent lease or resale (i.e., such as antique dealers).

This transitional rule is necessary because many of the used goods being sold after the GST implementation have not, themselves, been subject to GST on their original acquisition. Since the notional credit is established to limit cascading tax (i.e., GST charges imposed on GST inherent in an asset), the system would be providing bonuses to registered purchasers on acquisitions of used property from non-registrants. It is anticipated that the three-year transitional period will erode the potential for these unintended benefits.

When goods that have been the subject of a notional input tax credit are sold as exports (no GST payable on the sale because they are zero-rated), notional input credits previously enjoyed by the vendor will be recaptured. In the absence of a rule like this, the GST system would be effectively subsidizing export sales of used goods during the transition period, where many of the goods were purchased before GST was implemented.

This transitional provision applies until 1994 and when used goods are sold or specified tangible personal property is sold at a value that exceeds prescribed values. The vendor will have to pay GST in an amount equal to the lesser of:

- GST actually paid for the goods;
- The notional input tax credit considered to have been paid for the goods;
- The tax that would have been paid for the goods had they not been initially acquired tax free on the tax-free sale of a business (see "Sale of Business" later in this chapter for more details); or
- The tax that would have been payable had the sale been an ordinary taxable supply made in Canada.

For example, assume that an antique dealer bought a table in 1993 for $535 from a non-registrant and claimed a notional input tax credit of $35. On a subsequent export of the table, the dealer would be obligated to remit $35 of GST, as a recovery of the notional input. Note that this repayment will not be available as an additional credit in computing the period's GST liability.

Notional input tax credits are also available for returnable containers (e.g., pop bottles) that are purchased by a registrant from a non-registrant. The grocery store buys pop bottles without having to pay GST on the transaction. The notional input credit will again be equal to the amount paid for the returnable container multiplied by 7/107ths. Notional credits cannot, however, be claimed for returnable containers for zero-rated goods, such as milk bottles, that were not originally subject to GST charges. Note that restrictions will be placed on the input tax credits (real or notional) that can be claimed for that portion of the price of specified tangible personal property that exceeds prescribed amounts. That is, the regulations will set price limits on these "appreciating" assets.

When prices are paid that exceed these limits, GST inputs will be available only on the price paid up to the limit. This restriction will not, however, apply to museums, galleries or other institutions that acquire the property for the purposes of exhibition where admissions are charged to the public.

12. Used Automobiles

The four commandments of used-car transactions are:

1. Private individuals who sell used cars to other private individuals, both of whom are not registered, will not have to pay GST on the sale.
2. Used-car dealers who sell cars to private individuals who are not registrants will charge GST on the sale.
3. GST won't be payable on a used-car sale by a private individual who is not registered to a used-car dealer.
4. Used-car dealers who buy cars from private individuals who are not registered will be allowed to claim a notional GST input tax credit on the purchase. (Note that the transitional limitations on notional inputs for acquisitions before

1994 should not affect used-car dealers, who buy for the purposes of resale.)

The Federation of Automobile Dealer Associations of Canada (FADAC) lobbied the federal government vigorously on the different GST treatment afforded to private used-car sales and commercial used-car sales. The concerns were that GST would create a bias against the public buying used cars from dealers on the basis that they were more expensive because of the tax liability.

In reality, because of the notional input tax credit recovery by dealers who buy used cars from non-registrants and the real input credits available where the cars are purchased commercially, the GST on used cars sold by dealers would only be based on profit margins. That is, GST will represent a 7% charge on the difference between what the dealer bought the car for (less inputs) and what the car was sold for.

For example, assume that a dealer bought a used car from a non-registrant for $6,350, becoming entitled to a notional input tax credit of $415. On a subsequent sale of the car for $7,000, tax of $490 would be paid, for a total purchase price of $7,490. The true GST tax burden, however, is equal to the difference between the notional tax credit the dealer was entitled to claim and the GST paid on the actual sale: $490-$415 = $75.

Compare this to a private sale, which would cost a purchaser only $7,000. If both the dealer and the private sale were made at this price, the dealer sale would be $490 more expensive.

Before GST, if the dealer's mark-up was 9.2% on its cars, it would have to sell this one for the full $7,000. However, since the dealer received a notional input credit of $415 on the original purchase, it could afford to reduce the purchase price by that amount and still enjoy the same profit margin of 9.2%, thus selling the car for $6,585.

It would clearly be in the best interests of used car dealers to show exactly how much GST is really payable on their automobiles in order to dispel any public perception that the full purchase price of the car was subject to GST. However, it is unlikely that dealers will provide such explicit information because that will let the public know exactly what the dealer's mark-up is on a particular car. It's a dilemma that used-car dealers will have to work around.

Special limitations have been established for persons registered under GST who buy passenger vehicles for use as a capital property in a commercial activity (i.e., cars and vans). Registrants will not be allowed to claim input tax credits for that portion of the cost of the vehicle that exceeds $24,000 (determined before adding federal and provincial taxes).

The object of this limitation is to mirror the restrictions in the income tax system for capital cost allowance deductions. It can be expected that this limit will change as time goes on and will reflect changes in the income tax restrictions.

Note that maximum input tax credits will be available only for any car or other passenger vehicle when it was used exclusively in a registrant's commercial enterprise. For this purpose, exclusive means 90% use or more for qualifying activities.

When use is not exclusive, the registrant will be allowed a pro-rated input credit allowance based on the capital cost allowance deducted for the vehicle under the Income Tax Act. The effect of this approach is to allow input tax credits to be claimed over a period of years on the same basis and in relation to capital cost allowance deductions made for income tax purposes.

For example, assume that in 1992 a van is purchased by an individual for $20,000; it is used for business 55% of the time and 45% of the time for personal activities. The individual would be entitled to capital cost allowance at a rate of 30% on 55% of the cost of the van in the first year of ownership, reduced by 50% under the initial year acquisition rules. The calculation would be 1/2 x 30% x 55% x $20,000 = $1,650.

The $1,650 would then be multiplied by 7/107ths (= $107.94) to determine the applicable input tax credit for that fiscal year. In the second year, assuming use ratios were the same, the individual would be entitled to capital cost allowance of $3,027.75 and a GST input tax credit of $198.07.

Note that this rule will apply only when GST was payable on the initial purchase of the vehicle. If it is acquired in a non-taxable manner — bought from a non-registrant as used goods — the pro-rated input tax credits will not be available.

When a registrant sells a passenger vehicle that was being used as a capital property in a commercial enterprise, it will be able to recover the GST inputs originally paid to acquire the vehicle that were not claimed because of these limitations. For example, if in the first two years of ownership, only 30% of the inputs were claimed, the remaining 70% will be recovered on a sale in the third year. This also applies to taxes paid for improvements on the vehicle (i.e., repairs or additional equipment).

This rule is important to restrict double taxation by imposing GST on goods that have not been the subject of full input tax credit claims.

Four amounts will be considered in determining the input tax recovery that may be claimed on these sales. They are:

- The GST paid on the initial acquisition;
- Input credits claimed for the vehicle during ownership;
- The cost of the vehicle, including improvements, and
- The sale price received by the vendor.

In the context of these amounts, the total credit that can be claimed will be equal to the lesser of two amounts:

1. The difference between the GST paid for the original purchase of the vehicle and the input credits the registrant claimed prior to the subsequent sale, and
2. When the selling price on the subsequent sale is less than the original cost of the vehicle plus the cost of improvements (which will be the case more than not), an amount equal to the difference in GST paid and claimed, as determined under 1. above, reduced proportionately by a ratio of the selling price divided by the original cost of the vehicle, plus the cost of improvements.

Assume that a corporation buys a company car for an employee at a cost of $30,000 in 1992 ($2,100 of GST paid), and spends another $2,000 ($140 of GST paid) improving the car in 1993. In 1994 the car is sold for $18,000. The car was used exclusively in the course of commercial activities.

The corporation was entitled to claim input credits of $1,680 (i.e., 7% of $24,000), the maximum credit allowed for passenger vehicles. On the subsequent sale, the corporation was required to collect $1,260 of GST.

It would therefore be entitled to claim further input credits of the lesser of:

1. $2,100 (the original GST paid on the car) plus $140 (GST paid on the cost of improvements) minus $1,680 (GST credits claimed) = $560
2. $560 times [$18,000 (selling price) divided by $32,000 (original cost plus cost of improvements)] = $315.00.

The second amount would be available as an additional input tax credit to the corporation on the subsequent sale of the car.

The object of this exercise is to allow a recovery of restricted input credits in relation to the vehicle under the $24,000 cost cap. The input credits not recovered relate to the cost of the vehicle in excess of that amount.

When a vehicle was not used exclusively in the commercial enterprises of a registrant, GST does not have to be paid on a subsequent sale of the vehicle as a used property, and input credit recovery will not be available. Double taxation is avoided because full input credits were not available to the registrant during ownership.

A mechanism has been established to recapture input tax credits previously claimed by a corporation where the registrant has stopped using the vehicle exclusively in commercial activities. In these circumstances, the registrant will be deemed to have sold the vehicle for its fair market value in a taxable transaction.

GST will then be payable by the registrant, effectively recouping previous inputs claimed.

When the vehicle continues to be used for some commercial purposes after this change in exclusive use, the registrant will be entitled to the pro-rated input tax credit claims discussed above. Thus, some of the GST paid on the deemed sale will be recoverable.

Though these mechanisms are relatively complex, they are necessary to ensure that double taxation does not occur. The need for these rules is really based on the fact that passenger vehicles are an asset that are frequently used for a combination of commercial and personal activities.

It would not be fair to have the GST system subsidize personal use by allowing the recovery of full input tax credits. The $24,000 limitation on maximum input credits that are available is also necessary to ensure that acquisitions of luxury cars are not subsidized by the GST system.

13. Importing Goods

A particularly unfair feature of the federal sales tax system has been the favourable treatment available to imported goods compared to the application of the tax to goods manufactured in Canada (a problem that won't exist under GST). This has often provided imported goods with a price advantage in the Canadian marketplace that domestic manufacturers couldn't match. In some price-sensitive market sectors, the competitive advantage enjoyed by imported goods acted as an economic barrier to domestic manufacturers that could not match the pricing.

Structural flaws indigenous to the system have prevented the implementation of interim measures designed to resolve the inequitable application of federal sales tax to imported goods.

For example, assume that a retailer imports records at a landed cost of $5 each, incurring federal sales tax charges of $.675. The retailer, after incurring marketing and distribution costs of $1.80 per unit, sells the record to consumers for a retail price of $10.99.

Compare this to the record manufacturer in Canada, who produces a record for $4, incurs marketing and distribution costs of $1.80 and sells the record to a retailer for $7.50 (which again sells the record for $10.99). In these circumstances, federal sales tax would be based on the $7.50 sales price between the manufacturer and the retailer, which includes the marketing and distribution costs, for a tax liability of $1.0125 per unit. The advantage enjoyed by the importer is equal to $.3375. Multiply that advantage by one million units per year and the cost of this flaw in the federal sales tax system would be $337,500.

The flaw imposes a tax on the marketing and distribution costs of Canadian manufacturers, as well as that portion of profit margins that relate to wholesale and retail trade levels.

For years, marketing and distribution companies have been used by domestic manufacturers to overcome this problem. Manufacturers would sell their products to wholly owned subsidiaries for a base price plus a small profit margin. The subsidiary would then incur marketing and distribution costs and sell the goods for a price that included profit margins for the higher trade levels.

Federal sales tax would be paid only on the selling price between the manufacturer and the subsidiary. Subsequent costs and profit margins would not be subject to the tax. This mechanism allowed domestic manufacturers to compete with importers in certain markets.

The federal government tried to stop this type of planning several times, unsuccessfully. First the issue was taken to court, where Revenue Canada lost the case when the court found that a part of the legislation was unconstitutional.

Next, the Department of Finance tried to enact new legislation that would put an end to the practice by deeming the selling price by a related marketing and distribution company to be treated as the base price for federal sales tax purposes. The proposed legislation went through several drafts, but it was judged to be flawed and was finally rejected by the House of

Commons Finance Committee. Though the government vowed to return with a revised version of the legislation, this initiative was dropped in light of the impending implementation of the GST.

The GST removes any and all competitive advantages that imported goods enjoyed under the federal sales tax system. From a commodity taxation perspective, imported goods and domestically manufactured goods are taxed equally.

The players are now on a level playing field.

As a general rule, all goods imported into Canada are subject to GST, payable at the same time customs duties have to be paid (usually on release from bond or delivery at the border).

In technical terms, GST is to be paid and collected in accordance with the procedures established under the Customs Tariff, as if the tax were a "duty" levied under that tariff. This will allow GST payment and collection to be integrated into current practices employed by the importation industry with respect to duties and tariffs.

The general rule will not apply to zero-rated goods and certain other goods acquired for diplomats and various international organizations. Zero-rated goods include basic groceries, medical equipment and prescription drugs. Agricultural and fishery products are also excluded from the general rule.

When goods are imported by registrants, they will usually be allowed to claim input tax credits for the GST paid on importation. Non-registrants who import goods will not normally be able to recover these inputs.

GST will be based on the duty-paid value of the goods imported into Canada. The "duty-paid value" of goods is an excise tax-law concept that refers to the cost of goods, plus customs payable under the Customs Tariff, duty payable under the Special Import Measures Act and any other taxes (excluding GST) that might be payable under the Excise Tax Act.

In certain cases, goods will be granted a special value for GST purposes as prescribed by regulation. An example might be goods that are temporarily imported into Canada.

When the value of goods at the border is disputed, the Customs Act rules will apply, under which an official determination of the value can be made. Appeals from this determination will also be made under the Customs Act. Other appeals in relation to imports will be governed by the rules in the Excise Tax Act.

Imported goods held in "bond" under the authority of Canada Customs will not be subject to federal taxes or duties until released. When goods in bond are sold, GST will not apply, as the sale is considered to have been made outside Canada. These goods will, if released into Canada, be subject to GST in line with the ordinary rules respecting the imposition of tax on imports.

14. Importing Services: Intangible Personal Property

GST will impose tax on the importation of services on a commodity tax basis for the first time in Canada. Their nature, in comparison to goods, is fundamentally different and must therefore be addressed by slightly different rules.

"Imported taxable supply" is a defined term. It refers to the supply of services as well as intellectual property rights, such as patents and copyrights.

The supply must be made outside Canada to a resident Canadian who receives it for personal use or consumption in Canada. Alternatively, it is received in Canada for use in commercial enterprises or for resale. Supplies that are already subject to GST under different parts of the legislation are excluded from this definition, as are zero-rated supplies. A special category of non-taxable importations is also excluded. As a matter of definition, exempt supplies (such as financial services) are excluded from this treatment.

Unlike imported goods (where the tax is based on duty-paid values), GST is imposed on the value of the consideration paid or payable for the services of intangibles. GST will be payable on the earlier of the day the consideration for the supply is paid or becomes legally due.

When the importer is a registrant under GST, it reports the liability in the same reporting periods as the GST on domestic transactions is reported. Non-registrants must report GST on imports each calendar quarter.

Recipients of imported services or intangibles have to file returns for their transactions, remitting the GST with the return. Registrants with fiscal-year taxation periods must file returns within three months after the end of each period. In all other cases, the returns must be filed no later than one month after the end of a reporting period.

A separate rule has been established for supplies made between permanent establishments of a person inside and outside Canada (i.e., branches in Canada and the United States). Services and intangibles transferred from the non-resident branch to Canada will be treated as a taxable supply. The value of that supply will, however, be based on the amount that is used to determine the person's income under the Income Tax Act.

For example, if a United States parent corporation allocates head office expenses to a Canadian branch, the deduction allowed under the Income Tax Act in determining branch income will be the basis on which GST is determined. This rule is designed to avoid disparity between the interaction of the two systems of taxation.

15. Exporting Goods and Services

For decades, exports have not been as competitively priced as they might have been because of the inefficiencies of the federal sales tax system. Under that system, exported goods were exempted from the imposition of sales tax. However, it was often impossible to remove many hidden components of the tax. As a result, many exports were subject to a tax that was supposed to apply only to consumption of goods in Canada.

One of the major benefits of the GST is that it is intended to allow exports to be more competitively priced by removing any and all tax before goods are sold outside the country. This represents one of the fundamental reasons for the government adopting a multi-staged tax, which allows hidden taxes to be removed from exports.

Exports are treated as zero-rated supplies. That means GST is not payable on sales. However, input tax credits may be claimed on zero-rated export sales, unlike other non-taxable sales.

GST is intended to be imposed on taxable consumption in Canada. Exports are logically excluded from the tax as they are not, by their nature, consumed in Canada.

The general rule imposing GST on taxable sales also subjects zero-rated sales to tax. However, it imposes GST at a rate of zero.

The object of this mechanism is to allow zero-rated transactions to effectively escape the imposition of tax while, at the same time, being subject to all of the other rules in the system. In this way, the rules regarding input tax credits, including recovery methods, are available.

Supplies that are considered zero-rated are listed in Schedules included with the legislation (see Appendix). One part of those Schedules refers to exports and establishes a number of rules and conditions that must be complied with before the zero-rated characterization is available.

From a technical perspective, GST applies only to supplies made in Canada. Since exports are transactions conducted outside Canada, it is arguable that exports do not even have to be zero-rated.

In practical terms, when determining whether the supply of goods, services or intangibles may be characterized as exports, it will be necessary to determine whether the supply was made outside Canada. Where it was, the supply can be zero-rated as an export.

In general, a sale of goods will be considered to be made outside Canada when the goods are delivered (or are to be delivered) outside Canada or are otherwise made available to a recipient outside Canada. Goods supplied on another basis, such as a lease, will be considered to be made outside Canada if possession of the goods is provided to a recipient outside Canada.

Intangible personal property (i.e., intellectual property) will be considered to be supplied outside Canada when the property is used (or to be used) either wholly or partially out of the country. Further, the property cannot be used in Canada.

When the supply of intangible property relates to real property that is located outside Canada, or to tangible personal property that is ordinarily located outside Canada, the supply will be considered to be made outside the country.

When the intangible supply relates to a service that is to be performed wholly outside the country, the supply will be considered to be made outside the country.

When real property is supplied, or a service in relation to real property, it will be considered to be made outside Canada when the real property is located outside the country.

Services will be considered to be made outside Canada when they are wholly performed out of the country.

Special rules have been established for situations in which goods are supplied in Canada to a purchaser which, in turn, exports them. They may be zero-rated when three conditions are satisfied:

- The Canadian purchaser does not use, consume or supply the property in Canada, but rather exports it;
- The property is not subject to further processing. For example, it is not transformed or altered while in Canada, except to the extent that the processing is necessary to the export process and is incidental, such as refrigeration or packaging.
- The supplier who sells goods to purchasers in these circumstances keeps records that contain information about the export that are satisfactory to Revenue Canada and the purchaser does not use its own truck to export the goods.

Non-residents who buy goods in Canada and then effectively

export them when they leave the country will be entitled to recover any GST paid on those goods.

Excisable goods, such as beer, liquor and tobacco products, will be zero-rated for export only when they are exported in bond after supply to a recipient in Canada.

As a general proposition, goods that are returned temporarily to Canada for servicing, such as repairs under warranty by a manufacturer, will be zero-rated. Transportation services are subject to tax. However, supplies made to unregistered foreign operators of ships, aircraft and railways will be zero-rated to ensure that they are not at a disadvantage in comparison to domestic operators who can recover their GST inputs.

Emergency repair services made in Canada to property owned by a non-resident will be zero-rated when the non-resident is invoiced for the services outside the country. If a resident is invoiced, GST will be payable.

Special rules have been established for agents who provide services to non-residents for supplies made outside Canada. In general, the rules are designed to ensure that all of the supplies made outside Canada are zero-rated for GST purposes. Further, commissions charged by the agents will not be subject to GST on the basis that the services were provided outside Canada (see Agents, later in this chapter for more detail).

Advisory services provided to non-residents who are considering moving to Canada are zero-rated. Consulting or research services are included in this category. For example, legal advice to a non-resident's branch operations in Canada would be zero-rated.

Goods supplied by way of mail or common carrier to individuals outside Canada will be zero-rated. Goods supplied to individuals resident in Canada, however, will be subject to GST, even if the individual intends to subsequently export them.

Charities that export goods or services for charitable purposes outside Canada will be entitled to rebates where input tax credits were otherwise denied. The rebate is intended to fully relieve these exports from GST.

A rule has been established to deal with situations under which goods have been zero-rated for export but are, in fact, never exported. It applies when a carrier has been provided with a declaration by the shipper that the property is being exported. Where not exported, the carrier's services will not be subject to zero-rating. The carrier will not, however, be obligated to collect GST if it did not know, or could not have reasonably known, that the property was to be diverted to a Canadian destination. The shipper will remain liable for tax on the carrier's services.

Transitional rules have been introduced for exported used goods before 1994. The rules are necessary because many of the used goods exported in the first several years of the new system will not have been subject to GST. Without these rules, the GST system would effectively be subsidizing the export of used goods that have never been subject to the tax.

GST will be payable on used goods that are exported before 1994. Registrants will have to pay tax on the lesser of two amounts:

- The tax that was actually paid for the goods, the tax that was notionally treated as having been paid on the goods (see "Used Goods: General," earlier in this chapter for more details), or the tax that should have been paid on the goods had they not been acquired tax free on the sale of a business (see "Sale of a Business," later in this chapter for more details); or
- The tax that would have been payable had the supply been made under taxable circumstances in Canada.

Alternatively, specified tangible personal property such as art (see "Used Goods: General," earlier in this chapter for more detail) appreciates and, on export, will be subject to GST in certain circumstances. When the price paid for these goods exceeds the prescribed value, GST will be payable.

Since these goods appreciate, notional input credits claimed on export might exceed the consideration originally paid on acquisition, resulting in the recovery of more GST than was paid. Again, this rule is necessary to ensure that the GST system does not subsidize exports of specified tangible personal property that has appreciated in value from the date of purchase.

16. Non-Residents

As a general rule, GST is not payable on the supply of personal property or services made by a non-resident. It is, for this purpose, considered to be a supply made outside of Canada.

There are, however, several key exceptions to this rule.

Where a non-resident makes a supply of goods or services in the course of carrying on a business in Canada, GST will apply to the transactions in line with the general rules applicable to residents. Note that the non-resident will therefore be entitled to claim small supplier status where its annual sales do not exceed the $30,000 threshold (see "Registration" earlier in this chapter for more details).

Non-residents who solicit orders subsequently delivered through the mail or by courier to recipients in Canada will be subject to GST when the value of the property does not exceed $40. They are deemed to be carrying on business in Canada.

The focus of this rule is primarily magazine, book and periodical publishers outside Canada and other prescribed goods. It will force them to charge GST on their subscription sales in Canada. In this way, domestic subscription sales will not be placed at a competitive disadvantage.

When non-residents are registrants, supplies of their goods or services will be deemed to be made in Canada and will therefore be subject to GST. This will be advantageous to non-residents that want to claim input tax credits in relation to their Canadian sales.

Non-residents in the performing arts, as well as non-residents who provide or stage performances, exhibits, activities or events in Canada, at which admission or attendance fees are charged directly to the public will be subject to GST. The non-resident will have an obligation to collect and remit the GST within their fiscal period, or earlier should they intend to leave Canada prior to the end of that fiscal period (deemed to be the calendar month for these purposes).

It is clear that the supply of real property situated in Canada by a non-resident is subject to GST. This is an inherent consequence of the system and is not governed by specific rules. Where non-residents do supply real property situated in Canada, however, purchasers or recipients of the supply will have an obligation to remit the GST directly to the government in the following circumstances:

- On all real property sales by non-residents.
- On all sales of non-residential property to buyers who are registered under GST.
- On all sales of residential property to GST registrants. This will not, however, include individuals who are buyers.
- On all sales to GST registrants who are prescribed by regulation for this purpose.

These rules are considered necessary to avoid the compliance problems that are associated with collecting tax from non-residents who do not have permanent establishments in Canada. Without them, non-residents would be provided with too many opportunities to avoid GST remittance on real property sales.

As a general rule, corporations resident in Canada that enter into transactions with related non-residents (i.e., being part of the same corporate or control group) will have an obligation to file information returns regarding those transactions. They will have to provide Revenue Canada with information sufficient for several practices to be scrutinized (i.e., such as fair market value pricing).

The returns will have to be filed within six months from the end of the year in which the transactions occurred.

17. Employees, Employers, Partners

Salaries and wages are not subject to GST. There remain, however, a number of GST issues that relate to the employment situation (as well as to partnerships) that both employees and employers should to keep in mind.

Perhaps the most critical area is employee benefits. For income tax purposes, employee benefits are, for the most part, considered to be taxable in the hands of an employee who uses, consumes or otherwise enjoys the benefits as a result of employment.

GST will have implications in this area for both income and GST taxes.

As a general proposition, taxable benefits provided to employees by employers will be treated as a normal taxable supply for GST purposes. This will give rise, correspondingly, to a liability for GST in relation to the benefit. The employee will not have to pay the GST on the benefit. His or her employer will.

Employee benefits will therefore cost an employer more than cash compensation, since the GST remitted in relation to the benefit will not be recoverable to the employer as an input credit. This will logically provide employers with an incentive to avoid providing benefits and replacing them with cash compensation (bonuses) that do not give rise to a GST liability, which becomes a cost of providing the benefit.

On the other hand, employees will have to recognize the imputed GST charge in relation to the benefit as income for tax purposes. This is logical in light of the fact that obtaining the benefit independently of the employment situation would result in a GST liability. Therefore, the provision of a benefit that the recipient does not pay GST on must, by its nature, represent an additional benefit (i.e., the saved GST) that should be added to income. Benefits will therefore become more expensive for employees to receive from employers. An incentive to favour cash compensation over benefits is again present.

Note that these rules apply only to benefits that are required to be included in income pursuant to several provisions of the Income Tax Act. These include:

- The value of board, lodging or any other kind of benefit received or enjoyed by the employee in the year in the course of or by virtue of his or her office or employment, and
- Benefits that represent standby charges for employer-provided automobiles.

A special timing rule has been established for these situations. Employee benefits will, for the purposes of GST, be considered to have been conferred at the end of February in the year following the year in which the benefit was actually conferred.

The timing rule is intended to make it easier for employers who are required to calculate employee benefits for income tax purposes at the same time for a preceding taxation year.

GST won't be payable if the benefit was in relation to a supply that was exempt or that the employer was, for other reasons, not entitled to claim as an input tax credit. GST will also not apply when the employer providing the benefit is not a registrant (such as a small supplier).

These benefit rules will not apply to a passenger vehicle (or aircraft) owned by an individual or partnership that is not used exclusively in commercial enterprises. When the vehicle is owned by other types of registrants such as corporations or trusts (but not financial institutions), the rules will not apply unless it is used "primarily" in commercial enterprises. The reason is that the employer would have originally been denied input credits for the cost of the vehicle on the original acquisition in these situations .

An employer can elect to have GST excluded from benefits provided in relation to leased passenger vehicles (or aircraft) that are used less than 50% of the time in commercial enterprises. The same election is available for vehicles or aircraft purchased by financial institutions. When inputs were partially claimed for those assets, however, this election will result in recapture of the inputs.

When an employer pays an employee's expenses incurred in Canada by way of an allowance, a notional input tax credit may be claimed equal to 7/107ths of the allowance paid. This rule applies when the expenses were substantially all taxable to the employee and are deductible for income tax purposes. The object of this rule is to allow the employer to recover GST paid by the employee that would otherwise have been recovered as an input tax credit had the employer incurred the expenses directly.

A similar rule has been established for reimbursement of expenses. The employer will be considered to have paid the employee's expenses and will therefore be entitled to claim input credits for the supply.

Identical rules for these purposes apply to partnerships when the partnership either provides an allowance to a partner or reimburses expenses.

Notê that union dues (and similar payments to associations by employees) will generally not be subject to GST. This exception applies whether the dues are paid by an employer or an employee.

Dues paid to maintain professional standing (either by employees, employers or partners) as recognized by statute (i.e., such as status to practise law in a province) will also not be liable for GST. However, the professional organizations in question can elect to have all such dues treated as taxable supplies. In this way, its members can claim input credits in relation to those costs.

Given the unique nature of partnerships, special rules have been enacted to address the issue of whether partners, or the partnership as an entity, have to be registered for GST purposes. For this purpose, partnerships and not partners individually will be treated as the entity engaged in the commercial enterprise. Partners will therefore not need to register separately under the GST regime.

Corporations that are members of partnerships, and are registered under the system, will be treated as being engaged in a commercial enterprise of the partnership in relation to expenses incurred for a partnership activity. The corporation will accordingly be entitled to claim input tax credits on its own return for GST paid on purchases for the commercial enterprises of the partnership.

When employees are entitled to deduct expenses in computing their employment income under the Income Tax Act, they will, in some circumstances, be entitled to a rebate of the GST inputs incurred in relation to those expenses. The rebate applies to capital cost allowance for automobiles, aircraft and musical instruments used in employment, to the extent GST was paid for their acquisition. The rebate will be equal to the GST component of those expenses, determined by multiplying the capital cost allowance claimed by 7/107ths.

The rebate also applies to expenses that are deductible in computing the employee's income from employment. The rebate will, again, be equal to the amount of the deduction multiplied by 7/107ths. For example, if capital cost allowance claims of $4,500 were available to an employee in a taxation year, a GST rebate equal to $4,500 x 7/107 = $294.39 could be recovered. This rebate is not, however, available to employees of most financial institutions and non-registered employers.

Employees have up to four years from the end of the year to which the expenses and capital cost allowance relate to file returns for this GST rebate.

Perhaps the most interesting aspect of this rebate is that it is based on expenses and capital cost allowance that was "deductible" but not necessarily deducted for income tax purposes. Thus, it is arguable that the deductions need not have actually been claimed for income tax purposes in order for the rebates to be available.

Partners are given similar entitlement to GST rebates for expenses that were taxable, but for which inputs could not be claimed. This rebate is available to partners who are individuals and are members of GST registered partnerships. The rebate applies to expenses incurred outside the partnership that are nevertheless deductible in computing the partner's income from that source for income tax purposes.

An example might be an entertainment expense a partner in an accounting firm incurs to entertain a partnership client. Often, these expenses are not reimbursed by partnerships and the partner is entitled to deduct the cost in computing partnership income. The rebate will be equal to the expense multiplied by 7/107ths. The rebate will not, however, be available for expenses that do not relate to commercial activities of the partnership.

Rebates payable are limited explicitly to the amount of input tax credits that would have been available to the partnership had the expenses been directly incurred.

18. Agents

Agents are subject to GST in certain circumstances on the taxable supplies they provide for their principals, even though they are not the real suppliers of goods or services. To avoid the tax on the supplies they handle, some agents will have to change the way they do business.

In basic terms, an agent is someone who undertakes to represent a principal, whether buyer or seller, in a commercial transaction. In some cases, agents provide important administrative functions that would otherwise be difficult to arrange. A common example might be the trust company that administers self-directed registered retirement savings plans.

In other cases, agents bring anonymity to a deal. It is common business practice for an agent to act for an undisclosed principal. Lawyers frequently act as agents for undisclosed principals in any number of transactions, most frequently in ones involving real estate. Auctioneers often act as agents for undisclosed vendors for the goods that they auction to the public on commission.

In the commercial world, agents are usually creatures of

contract. It is only in government that agencies are most often created by statute to carry out sovereign objectives. As a result, the diversity of agency relationships is infinite. Agencies are so prevalent in the commercial world that the public often does not even know (nor care) that it is dealing with one. That's what will give agents headaches under the GST.

Special rules have been established for any registrants under the system who, in the course of a commercial activity, make a supply of property or services on behalf of a person (described as a vendor) to a recipient. As a general rule, the agent will be considered to have made the supply to the recipient. That means the agent will be obligated to collect GST on the supply and remit it to the government. It also means that the agent will be considered to have received the supply from the vendor (the agent's principal) giving rise to a GST liability between them.

At the same time, agents will be entitled to claim input tax credits on the GST paid to acquire the goods or services from their principals. Auctioneers acting for undisclosed vendors would be entitled to the notional input tax credits available on the sale of used goods.

Take an extreme example: an agent acting for an aircraft manufacturer with a Canadian base sells a Canadian airline a 747 jumbo jet (current price about $150 million). The airline would be obligated to pay $10.5 million in GST to the agent on the sale. In turn, the agent would be obligated to pay tax to the manufacturer equal to 7% of the cost of the aircraft less the agency fee. Though fees can be high on aircraft sales, they represent only a small percentage of the actual sale price. Assuming a fee of $1,000,000, the agent would have a $10.43-million GST liability on the transaction.

Though the agent will ultimately recover its full tax liability under the system, the process can take time. If the purchase, sale and payment for the aircraft is not carefully orchestrated, the agent could find itself liable to pay more than $10 million to its principal that it might not recover for weeks, or even months, after.

It's doubtful that any agents will want to finance a major portion of GST to a principal for any length of time, if at all.

The solution is to make it clear that the agency exists. When one of three conditions is satisfied, GST will be payable once, by the recipient to a vendor, and the only tax an agent will see is the 7% added to the cost of its services.

No GST liability will arise when:

- The agent entered into an agreement with the recipient as a representative for a vendor;
- The agent issued a receipt or invoice for the supply in the vendor's name, or
- The agent failed to disclose in writing that the vendor is not a registrant under the system.

Agents will want to be careful how they conduct business under the GST regime. When agencies are not disclosed, the agents could find they have serious cash-flow problems when they are deemed to have acquired all of the supplies provided by their clients. Cash flows will be most strained when accounts by recipients are not promptly paid, extending financing periods during which GST is not recovered by the agents.

Agents who supply services for non-residents are treated differently. The general rule provides that supplies procured by an agent for a non-resident principal will be considered not to have been made in Canada (therefore not attracting GST liability).

Further, the agent's charges to the non-resident are considered to have been made outside Canada. They are, accordingly, not subject to GST. Thus, for example, travel agents that earn commissions from non-residents by booking accommodation outside Canada will not have to account for GST on those commissions.

By the operation of several rules relating to supplies considered to have been made outside Canada, agents' commissions earned on those supplies on behalf of non-resident principals will also be free of GST. Thus, booking agents for non-resident performers will not have to charge GST on their commissions. Similarly, customs brokers providing customs-broking services to non-residents will not have their commissions subjected to GST.

19. Food, Beverage and Entertainment Expenses

The recovery of GST inputs for food, beverage and entertainment expenses will be limited, as those expenses are limited as deductions for income tax purposes. The Income Tax Act imposes proportionate limitations on the ability of taxpayers to claim the full cost of food, beverage and entertainment expenses incurred in relation to a business activity as a deduction in computing income from that source. The limitations were introduced for those expenses incurred after June 17, 1987, as part of the government's first phase of income tax reform.

The limitations reduce the amount that a taxpayer may claim to 80% of the expenses otherwise incurred. The remaining 20% represents a non-deductible expense.

This limitation will not apply in five situations:

- When the taxpayer was in the business of providing the food, beverage or entertainment for compensation in the ordinary course of business;
- When the expenses relate to a fund-raising event, where the primary object is the benefit of a registered charity;
- When the taxpayer is compensated for the expense;
- When the expense has to otherwise be included in an employee's income, or
- When an employer incurs the expense for food, beverages or entertainment that are generally available to employees at a particular location.

Note that an allocation for these expenses will be deemed to be made for convention or seminar fees when food is provided to participants. In these circumstances, if the organizers do not show an allocation for food on the fee receipt, $50 will be deemed to be the cost of the food, only 80% of which will be deductible in accordance with this rule.

Note also that amounts paid for travel, whether on an airplane, train or bus, will be considered to be, in part, amounts paid for food, beverages or entertainment. This is a pragmatic exception since it would be impossible to distinguish between the different services available in these circumstances that might be technically caught by this rule.

GST input tax credit limitations are also imposed on the cost of food, beverages and entertainment. The limitations are intended to mirror restrictions on deductibility imposed by the Income Tax Act. In these circumstances, only 80% of the GST paid for these supplies will be available as a credit.

For ease of accounting, a registrant will be allowed to claim full input tax credits during the course of a year and recapture the 20% balance at the end of the year. The 20% recapture will be added to the vendor's net tax amount at the end of the year. The object is to allow vendors to calculate their net input credits for these supplies at the same time they can be calculated for income tax purposes.

It is important to note that the exceptions contained in the Income Tax Act to the application of this limitation will apply equally for the purposes of the GST input restriction.

20. Capital Personal Property: Changes in Use

Capital personal property includes any property that would qualify as a capital property for income tax purposes. The Income Tax Act defines a capital property as one that, on its disposition, would give rise to either a capital gain or capital loss.

Although this definition clearly includes depreciable assets, certain exclusions have been incorporated into the definition for

GST purposes. Capital property is defined to exclude assets included in Classes 12 (deductible at a rate of 100%) and 14 (intangible personal property, such as patents and copyrights) of Schedule II to the Income Tax Act.

Capital personal properties are what make the business world go round. They are the assets, equipment, machinery and even buildings in which commercial activities are conducted, housed or facilitated.

There is a fundamental difference between the treatment afforded to capital personal property in comparison to capital real property.

Input tax credits will be available for capital personal property only when it is used primarily in a commercial enterprise. With real property, inputs may be pro-rated between commercial and non-commercial uses.

In some cases, it is difficult to distinguish between capital personal property and real property, for instance when a piece of equipment is attached to a building. In these circumstances, Revenue Canada is given the authority to make a determination for GST purposes. The rule is necessary in order to ascertain whether an allocation of input credits is available, or whether they are restricted because the property is not used primarily in a commercial enterprise.

A system has been developed in the legislation to deal with changes in use of property. Without an organized approach to this issue, it would be easy for taxpayers to buy assets for commercial use, claim input credits and then change the use of their property to non-commercial enterprises without having to recapture the input credits. This would result in GST subsidizing non-commercial activities, a result that contravenes the spirit and object of the tax.

When a registrant buys or otherwise acquires personal capital property, input credits will be available if it is intended that the asset be used for qualifying purposes. The rules specifically state that it is this intention that will represent the basis upon which input credits can be claimed in these circumstances. Should the use of the capital personal property at some point actually be different than the stated intention (i.e., the property is used for another purpose), the change-in-use rules will apply to recapture input credits previously claimed.

In order not to make matters impossible for circumstances in which the property is used sporadically for non-commercial purposes (i.e., a computer is occasionally used to prepare personal letters), an "insignificant change in use" rule is established. Under this rule, insignificant changes in use will not result in the application of the change-in-use rules and corresponding recapture of input tax credits. Rather, the property will continue to retain its existing characterization for GST purposes.

An insignificant change is defined to mean a change of less than 10% in use. Note that this test is subjective and that changes in use may mean that actual use has changed by 10% of time used. Alternatively, the change may relate to the time the asset is available for use, as opposed to actually being used.

When the change in use represents a change from one primary use to another primary use, the change-in-use rules will apply, regardless of the fact that the primary change represents less than 10% of a change. For example, an author who has finished a book uses his computer only for the occasional letter and buys a new computer for the next book he is to write. In these circumstances, though change of use of the first computer may be less than 10%, the primary use for the computer (i.e., book writing vs. letter writing) has changed, attracting application of the change-in-use rules.

The general rule states that when a capital personal property is acquired or imported for primary use in a commercial activity, input credits may be claimed by the registrant on the property. The term "primarily" is defined to mean more than 50%.

When this 50% test is met, the property will be considered to have been used "exclusively" in the commercial enterprise, attracting full input credits. As stated above, no credits can be claimed when exclusivity is not established.

Note that these rules do not apply to financial institutions. They also do not apply to passenger vehicles or aircraft owned by partnerships or self-employed individuals.

Two different types of change-in-use rules have been enacted. The first type deals with registrants who begin to use capital personal property primarily in a commercial enterprise. In these circumstances, the registrant will be entitled to claim input credits not previously available for the property (i.e., it was first acquired for non-commercial purposes).

The second type deals with situations in which property that was used for commercial purposes either ceases to be used altogether or is used for non-qualifying purposes. In these situations, previously claimed inputs will have to be repaid.

When capital property (not previously subject to an input credit claim) starts to be used primarily (more than 50%) in a commercial activity, input credits can be claimed where GST was originally paid on the asset. Note that if the property was acquired before GST was implemented, no credits can be claimed in spite of an increase in use.

The inputs that may be claimed will be equal to the lesser of two amounts:

- All GST previously paid in relation to the property, including GST paid on improvements to same. This will include taxes considered to have been paid as a result of a deemed disposition of the property as a consequence of a decrease in its commercial use below the 50% threshold.
- The GST that would be payable had the property been acquired for its fair market value at the time the change occurred.

This rule is necessary to ensure that inputs in excess of fair market value of depreciating assets are not recovered inadvertently.

Note that the change-of-use rules for real property (see

Chapter IV, "Real Property," for more detail) are different, in that a proportionate recovery of input credits is available in relation to the percentage in the change in use.

When property that has been the subject of input credit claims as a consequence of being used primarily in commercial activities ceases to be so used, the registrant will be considered to have made a taxable supply of the property at that time equal to its fair market value. In this way, the value of the property results in a deemed GST liability that must be remitted to the government in the ordinary course. This puts the registrant in a position identical to any person who acquired the property at that time for its fair market value.

Thus, for example, if a property had a fair market value of $5,000 at the time its use changed, the registrant would be obligated to remit $350 to the government on account of GST. This remittance cannot subsequently be claimed as an input credit by the registrant.

Should the registrant subsequently sell the property, no further GST liability will arise. This is accomplished by deeming the subsequent sale not to be a taxable supply for GST purposes.

Note again that these rules do not apply to financial institutions nor passenger vehicles or aircraft owned by partnerships or self-employed individuals.

Several special rules have been established for particular situations.

A registrant that is not a financial institution, but that provides financial services, will not be prohibited from claiming input credits for property acquired for those operations. This is in contrast to financial institutions that cannot claim credits for assets acquired for their exempt activities.

Musical instruments owned by individuals who are registrants will be considered to have been used in a commercial enterprise when used both in employment and in a partnership in which the individual is a member. For example, when the instrument is used 25% of the time in self-employment as a musician and 75% of the time as an employee in a symphony orchestra, full input credits will be available.

Note also that musicians who are not registrants will nevertheless be able to recover inputs on their instruments by way of a special rebate established for that purpose (see "Rebates," later in this chapter, for more detail).

21. Bad Debts

GST is payable to the government the earlier of the time the liability becomes payable, or is actually paid. That means GST is payable on receivables. Therefore taxpayers will often have to remit GST long before they are paid by the recipient of their supply.

What happens when recipients never pay?

The GST will be recovered through a bad debt credit in the system. As a general rule, when a registrant writes off a receivable as a bad debt for income tax and accounting purposes, a corresponding deduction can be made. It will result in the recovery of the GST previously remitted for the original receivable.

The deduction may be claimed either in the reporting period in which the bad debt was written off, or in a reporting period that ends no later than four years from the end of the period in which the write-off was taken.

The bad debt deduction will be equal to 7/107ths of the amount written off. It can be claimed as a deduction from a registrant's net tax amount for the period in which the bad debt was recognized.

When a registrant's net tax amount is positive, the GST component of a bad debt will effectively be recovered from GST collected on supplies made in that period. When the net tax amount is negative, the registrant will have to recover the tax as a refund.

As a practical matter, this will provide businesses with an incentive to write off bad debts as soon as possible, in order to limit exposure to lengthier financing of the GST component of a receivable.

Should the bad debt ever be recovered, the inherent GST component will have to be remitted in the ordinary course.

22. Rebates

The most efficient multi-stage tax system (i.e., the one that is easiest to comply with and has the fewest deficiencies) is one that applies universally, without exception.

A tax system that has no exceptions is, however, an unattainable fantasy in light of political, social and economic realities in a modern world. Thus, the GST was designed to provide exceptions to itself in three fundamental ways. The methods employed for this purpose include exemption, zero-rating and full taxation.

Under an exemption method, the registrant pays GST on its purchases and does not charge tax on sales. Thus, tax is not directly recovered, but might indirectly be recovered through increased prices. In this way, the registrant becomes the consumer of tax, being unable to reclaim any taxes paid.

Conversely, under a zero-rating method, the registrant pays tax on its purchases and is deemed to charge tax on sales, but at a rate of zero. This entitles the registrant to a credit for input taxes. The zero-rating method of excepting GST normally has the least impact, in practical terms, in comparison to the other methods.

Finally, with a full taxation method, all sales are entirely subject to tax and the registrant is entitled to recover input taxes. The purchaser then recovers GST by way of a tax-rebate scheme.

The rebate system allows purchasers or recipients of taxable supplies to go into the marketplace and acquire goods and services with the least possible impact from a compliance perspective. They are treated like any other purchaser by a vendor, which is not required to attempt to segregate sales based on a category of buyer. To require segregation in these circumstances would make the system virtually impossible to comply with and would create an abundance of opportunities to circumvent the rules. Nevertheless, rebates have been provided to several types of purchasers and for several types of transactions to save various classes of recipient from the burdens of GST. In some cases, the rebates are available as a matter of public policy (e.g., charities). In other cases, they are available as a matter of economic reality (e.g., the tourist trade would be severely affected without a rebate).

Note that some rebates will reimburse full GST burdens (such as tourist rebates), while others will reimburse only partial tax charges (such as charitable rebates).

Thus, purchasers entitled to rebates pay the full GST inputs for purchases and apply to the government for recovery of some or all of those inputs. The following is a list of rebates and some of the conditions that must be satisfied in order for applicants to recover their inputs (note that rebates for residential homes are discussed in Chapter IV, "Real Estate," which should be referred to for more detail):

a. Non-Residents: Tourists

As a general rule, non-residents who buy goods in Canada will be entitled to obtain a rebate of GST paid for the goods after they have taken the goods out of the country. The goods acquired have to be tangible personal property for use primarily outside Canada. Specified tangible personal property (i.e., appreciating assets like art, antiques or jewellery) bought for value that exceeds values prescribed by regulation will not qualify for this purpose. Neither will alcohol or tobacco products, nor automotive gas or oil.

Presumably other consumables will qualify, such as bug spray or hand cream, where it is intended that they be used primarily outside Canada. Revenue Canada may deny some claims in the absence of evidence of primary use.

A number of conditions must be satisfied in order for the rebate to be given:

- The applicant must apply for the rebate within one year after receipt of the supply. The application must be made on a prescribed form.

- The rebate applied for must exceed $25.
- Limits are placed on the number of applications that can be made in a period. When applicants are individuals, only one claim per calendar quarter can be made. For others, only one claim per calendar month can be made. In practical terms, this will cut down the number of returns that the government will have to deal with annually in order to administer this rebate.
- The applicant must be a non-resident at the time the application was made.

GST paid on accommodation, such as motels, hotels and similar short-term rentals, will also be recoverable to non-residents. Note that short-term accommodation is limited to 30 days per visit for this purpose.

When the cost of short-term accommodation is built into the cost of a tour package, rebates will be available on an allocated basis in accordance with formulas established under the regulations. Actual tax paid on accommodation can be recovered in these circumstances where these charges can be separately identified.

This is a critical rebate for the tourist industry. Some observers have suggested that even with the rebate, tourism will suffer a psychological blow under GST. Without a rebate mechanism of this sort, the blow could have been fatal to the industry.

b. Employees and Partners

This rebate has been discussed in detail earlier in this chapter ("Employees, Employers, Partners"). In general, employees and partners will be entitled to obtain rebates for expenses incurred in the course of their activities of employment or partnership.

The rebates will be available for expenses that are deductible in computing the employee's or partner's income from those sources under the Income Tax Act. These include expenses relating to automobiles and aircraft and musical instruments or equipment, such as home computers.

Rebates will be equal to 7/107ths of the expenses. They will be available for up to four years from the end of the year in which the expenses were incurred for income tax purposes.

Note that this rebate will not be available for employees of certain financial institutions.

c. Charities, Non-Profit Organizations and Public Service Bodies

Charities and non-profit organizations (substantially funded by governments) will be entitled to a rebate of 50% of their GST inputs. The "MUSH" sector (municipalities, universities, schools and hospitals) will also be entitled to rebates of a prescribed (by regulation) proportion of their GST input taxes.

The theory behind these rebates is that these organizations be subject to tax at roughly the same levels that were imposed under the federal sales-tax system. GST is not intended to become an additional burden to them.

At the same time, recipients of most supplies of goods or services from these organizations will not be subject to tax. This effect was considered necessary for public policy reasons in many cases.

Note that the definition of charities includes non-profit nursing homes, whether or not they are registered as a charity under the Income Tax Act.

Rebate claims by organizations that are registrants are to be made in their ordinary reporting periods. Non-registrants will be entitled to make claims either annually or one every fiscal quarter. It is advisable for these organizations to make quarterly claims in order to improve their cash flows.

Municipalities (defined by regulation) will be entitled to rebates only for the supply of municipal services. Transit systems that are distinct from municipalities will be able to obtain the same characterization in order to be entitled to the rebates available to their municipalities.

Qualifying non-profit organizations will be those that enjoy government funding of at least 40%. This will apply only to direct financial assistance from any of the three levels of government. It will not, for example, include low-interest loans or guarantees.

Organizations will be entitled to claim rebates as soon as they have satisfied eligibility criteria. GST inputs incurred in a year but before the criteria is satisfied will nevertheless be recoverable for that year.

Organizations will have up to four years from the end of the period in which inputs are incurred to make rebate claims.

Rebates will not be available for certain prescribed purchases. These include alcohol and tobacco, as well as new goods purchased solely for resale, including alcohol and tobacco.

In order to simplify rebate accounting, a simplified method is available to charities, the MUSH sector and non-profits. This is necessary because these organizations can have taxable activities, for which full rebates may be claimed, as well as activities that are subject to rebate, on which input credits are denied.

It can become impossible to segregate between purchases on an actual tax-paid basis. For example, allocations would have to be made on a subjective basis, such as determining how the cost of a typewriter (or for that matter, pens and paper) must be divided between taxable and rebateable activities.

Under this method, the organization will be able to claim input credits for inventories and purchases of capital goods or real property (over $10,000). For rebateable purchases, rebates will be available on the basis of a prescribed percentage of taxable sales.

All of these formulas and mechanisms are to be established by the regulations.

The method is elective and may be chosen by an organization for the reporting period in which it is to become effective by filing an election form with the return for that period. Elections can be revoked in a similar manner. Note that the election is available only for organizations and charities that are registered for GST (i.e., they are the only ones that will claim input credits along with rebates). If registration is revoked, the election for simplified accounting will also be deemed to have been revoked.

The rebate percentages are vital to these entities. In light of their sensitive nature, the legislation has been drafted in such a way that they cannot be changed by regulation. Thus, only an Act of Parliament (such as an amending bill in a budget) can effect changes to the rates.

A special rebate is available for charity exports, to the extent that the entity was not otherwise entitled to an input credit for the supply. The rebate will be equal to the full GST inputs (rather than 50%) in order that the exports not be subject to tax (in line with the scheme of the legislation regarding exports).

For greater certainty, rules are established to ensure that rebates are not claimed for the same supply more than once and that overpayments by the government are to be repaid by a recipient.

When a tax payment has been made in error, the remittance can be recovered as a rebate. The assessment and appeal procedures under the Customs Act (rather than the GST legislation) will, however, have to be followed to obtain this rebate.

23. Bankruptcies, Receiverships, Seizures, Repossessions and Foreclosures

Creditors could see the value of their security reduced when the proposed GST applies on a forfeiture, seizure or repossession of goods. Debtors, on the other hand, will be able to recover input tax credits even though they have defaulted. In the end, however, the system will make everything work out right.

Most transactions involving the sale of goods without full payment, or the lending of money to make purchases, give creditors the right to seize or repossess property. Thousands of times each day, taxpayers put deposits down to buy goods or services, signing agreements that allow the vendor to keep the deposit if the buyer fails to complete the contract.

The range of these situations is extensive.

Take, for example, car sales. Except when cash is paid, buying a car usually involves arranging to finance the purchase under terms that allow the creditor, whether a dealership or a bank, to repossess the vehicle if payments are not made.

On the commercial side, equipment sales are usually subject to chattel mortgages that allow a vendor or creditor to seize the secured property. As well, millions of dollars of deposits are forfeited each year when transactions go sour.

GST will apply to many of these situations in different ways. If creditors are not careful, they could find their net returns reduced by GST.

Forfeitures are the best illustration of this problem. As a general rule, when an amount is forfeited as a consequence of a breach or cancellation of an agreement for the provision of a taxable supply, the creditor will be treated as having made the supply.

The result is that GST will be payable on the forfeited amount. The government will consider that GST is included in the forfeiture and the creditor will be able to keep only 100/107ths of the amount.

Assume that a $100,000 deposit has been forfeited on an equipment sale. If GST is considered to be included in the deposit, the net selling price will be estimated to be $93,457.90 and the balance, $6,542.10, will be regarded as the tax component.

While the vendor remits the $6,542 as GST, the failed purchaser would be entitled to recover that amount as an input tax credit. That will allow the purchaser to offset the credit against taxes it has collected on sales, or apply for a direct refund.

The practical effect is that the vendor's deposit has been reduced by the hypothetical GST. The issue is whether vendors should consider asking for higher deposits to take the GST effect into account.

Special rules have also been proposed for seizures and repossessions. In general terms, GST will not apply when property has been seized or repossessed from a registrant (i.e., commercial taxpayer) to satisfy a debt or obligation, or under a general power to seize by way of contract. This is a logical rule, because GST would have been paid on the original transfer. When the seized property is subsequently resold, GST would be applied in the normal course.

When the property is sold by a court, however, GST will not apply because the sale will not be considered to have been made in the course of a commercial activity. As a result, court-ordered receivership sales may now carry the extra bonus of being made on a GST-free basis.

When a creditor uses repossessed property for its own operations, it will be considered to have received a taxable supply and will be required to pay GST on a notional price equal to the fair market value of the property.

Finally, if property is repossessed from a non-registrant (i.e., a consumer), the creditor will become entitled to a notional input tax credit. This rule addresses the fact that the consumer paid GST on the original purchase but did not recover the tax as an input credit as a commercial operation would have. When this rule applies, it should have the effect of increasing the gross recovery to a creditor by the amount of the GST tax credit.

When an insurer acquires property as settlement of an insurance claim, no GST will be payable because the transfer is considered to have been made for no consideration. A subsequent sale of the property by an insurer will, however, be taxable in the ordinary course, unless the supply is zero-rated or exempt. If an insurer uses the property instead of selling it, GST will be payable on its fair market value at the time its use begins. The insurer will have to remit the imputed GST for that reporting period.

Insurers will, in some circumstances, be able to claim input credits for the property they begin to use, when the use is in a commercial enterprise. When the use is for exempt purposes, credits will not be available.

If the insurer obtains the property from a non-registrant and resells it, full input credits will be available. This rule is necessary to avoid double taxation.

As a general rule, GST will not be payable on the transfer of property on either the declaration of a bankruptcy, or on a discharge from a bankruptcy. The trustee in bankruptcy is treated as an agent of the bankrupt. Trustees will, however, have obligations to administer the GST liabilities and obligations of the bankrupt estate in accordance with the legislation.

Similar rules have been established for receivers, receiver-managers, liquidators or committees that are appointed to either manage, operate or liquidate the commercial affairs of a person.

24. Death and Estates

As with income tax, death attracts consequences from GST. Special rules have been established to deal with the peculiar circumstances that arise in these situations from a commercial perspective.

The rules apply to "executors" of an individual. An executor is the administrator of an estate, or any other person responsible under applicable law for the collection, administration and disposition of the deceased's property, as well as for the payment of debts from the proceeds realized on the disposition of the property and the distribution of the balance to beneficiaries.

In general, property passing to an executor of an estate as a consequence of the death of an individual will be considered to have been transferred for no consideration. Therefore, GST will not be payable on that transfer. The executor will be deemed to be using the property for the same purposes that it was used by the deceased prior to death (i.e., whether commercial or personal).

The executor will also be deemed to have paid tax on the

property that was originally paid by the deceased and to have collected any input credits that were claimed by the deceased.

The net effect of these deeming provisions is to allow the executor to step into the deceased's shoes for GST purposes and have the system apply as it normally would to the assets and property of an estate. Executors should note that they will be subject to all of the obligations and liabilities of the legislation in their dealings with the assets of a deceased's estate, as the deceased would have been.

25. Prizes and Competitions

Luck is about to be taxed. And although the cost of bets, games of chance and prizes will go up, winning will still be tax free.

Those who operate games of chance, including races, and take bets are subject to GST in a unique way. Rules have been established with the objective of subjecting the operator's profit margin to tax. In this way, the value of the services provided by the operator are subject to GST.

Vendors who take bets will be deemed to have supplied services to bettors. The value of that supply is to be determined in accordance with the following formula:

$$A \times (B - C)$$

In this formula, A represents the consideration fraction; B is the amount of the bet and C is tax imposed by the federal or provincial government in relation to the bet (such as provincial sales tax).

Through this formula, the provincial sales taxes are removed from the base for determining GST liability.

For example, assume that a bet placed by a participant in a game of chance is $12, including provincial sales tax at 10%. Without sales tax, the bet would have a base cost of $10.90.

In this example, the operator would be deemed to have

collected GST on the bet equal to 71¢, determined by multiplying $10.90 by 100/107ths. That amount would have to be remitted to the government as GST on the bet.

On the other side of the equation, when an operator pays out winnings to a bettor or participant in a game of chance (such as bingo), there will be a deemed taxable supply, giving rise to notional input credits (determined by multiplying the winnings by 7/107ths).

In this way, the difference between the amounts collected on bets or admission to games of chance and the amounts paid out as winnings (i.e., the operator's margin) will be subject to GST.

The economic consequence of these rules is that the cost of bets and games of chance to consumers will increase by the GST imposed on an operator's profit margins.

Separate rules have been established for prizes won in competitive events. When a registrant's commercial enterprises include organizing, promoting, hosting or otherwise staging a competitive event, prizes awarded to winning competitors will not be treated as a taxable supply. Thus, GST need not be paid by the winners in the competition.

The registrant organizer will, however, not be entitled to claim input credits for any prizes, particularly if they are property awards (i.e., a new set of golf clubs).

Contributions made towards a prize purse by participants in a competitive event will not be considered to be a taxable supply. Thus, GST will not be payable on the contribution. However, contributions that are identified as entrance fees will be subject to GST as an ordinary admission charge.

26. Sale of Business

An exception to the ordinary rules regarding the application of GST to the taxable supply of goods or services is available when all or substantially all of the assets of a business are sold. In these circumstances, the parties can elect to have GST not apply to the transfer.

When control of corporations is transferred by way of a share sale, GST will not apply because the transfer of securities is not generally subject to the tax. It would be particularly unfair to force parties that sold assets, rather than shares of a corporation, to pay GST on the sale when similar liabilities were not imposed on share sales.

In order to avoid the artificial steps of incorporating companies, transferring a business and selling shares to avoid GST, an election is provided where the parties decide that that course is preferable.

The election will be available when registrants sell or transfer all or substantially all of the assets used in a business (which qualifies as a commercial activity for GST purposes) as a going concern. As long as both the vendor and purchaser are registrants, they will be entitled to elect to have the transaction not subjected to GST.

Note that the purchaser will be deemed to have acquired the assets for use exclusively in the course of a commercial enterprise. This rule is necessary for the purpose of the change-in-use rules that apply to capital property. In this way, the purchaser will be considered to have paid tax on the assets (even though no tax was actually paid) and the change-in-use rules will allow the recovery of inputs in the ordinary course of the application of those rules.

This election will probably be most useful when the payment of GST would have adverse cash-flow consequences to a purchaser. For example, when the purchaser was a zero-rated food manufacturer, GST paid on the acquisition of another business would be recovered only by way of refund from the government.

Depending on the fiscal reporting period of the purchaser, it could be months before the GST paid on the acquisition was recovered, during which time the purchaser would be financing the GST inputs on the acquisition.

27. Appropriation of Property: Shareholder Benefits

Diverting goods and services from commercial enterprises to personal use will result in a GST liability (not to mention the income tax implications arising from recognizing tax evasion).

Without this rule, registrants who are individuals could exploit the GST system by acquiring goods and services in commercial activities, recovering input credits and diverting them to personal use without having to pay the GST that would otherwise be incurred had the supply been acquired for personal use originally.

When a diversion of this kind occurs, the individual will be treated as having self-supplied the goods or services at their fair market value at the time of the diversion. In this way, GST will be payable and must be remitted by the registrant in the ordinary course for their fair market value. Note that this rule will not apply to the appropriation of capital personal property, which is the subject of its own distinct scheme under the legislation (see "Capital Personal Property," earlier in this chapter for more details).

A similar self-supply rule applies when property is appropriated (i.e., diverted from a commercial to a personal use) by a corporation for the benefit of a shareholder or by a partnership for the benefit of a partner. It also applies when property is appropriated by a trust for the benefit of a beneficiary or by charities and non-profit corporations that are registrants for the benefit of their members.

In these circumstances, GST will be deemed to arise in respect of the fair market value of the property appropriated at the time of the diversion.

Both of these self-supply rules will not apply when the supply appropriated was not originally subject to input credits on the basis of original personal use being high in relation to the supply. This rule limits the double taxation that would occur when inputs were not originally available and GST arises on a subsequent diversion, basically subjecting the supply to tax twice.

Another self-supply rule exists for cases where shareholders of corporations receive benefits that are subject to recognition as income under the Income Tax Act. These benefits arise when any form of benefit has been conferred by a corporation on a shareholder, or to a person in contemplation of their becoming a shareholder.

In these circumstances, not only will the value of the benefit be recognized as income for tax purposes, but the value of an imputed GST liability will also have to be taxed under the Income Tax Act. The imputed GST liability will be based on the amount that had to be recognized as a benefit for income tax purposes. The registrant conferring the benefit (i.e., the corporation) will be obligated to remit the imputed GST liability in line with the normal rules.

28. Travel

A mechanism had to be developed to exclude GST from the cost of those portions of a travel or tour package that should not otherwise be subject to the tax had the consumer purchased the travel services directly.

For this purpose, a special formula has been devised (in Part VI of Schedule VI – Zero-Rated Property and Services — see Appendix for details) to deal with the distinctions that must be made in these situations.

The formula operates to zero-rate the non-taxable part of a tour package. This might include food, travel outside Canada and accommodation outside Canada.

Tour operators are required to make an allocation of the cost of their packages to a purchaser based on a pro-ration of their selling prices according to the relative values of the non-taxable and taxable portions of the tour. The pro-ration will be based on the cost of each component of the package to the tour operator.

This has the effect, as well, of imposing GST on the operator's profit margins inherent in the package.

For example, assume that a tour operator has an average net cost (after claiming input credits) of $600 on a round-trip flight (which is taxable) from Vancouver to Los Angeles; accommodation with entertainment (which is zero-rated) is $900. Also assume a 10% mark-up as profit for the operator.

In this case, the cost of the taxable portion of the package represents 40% of the total cost of the package, with the zero-rated portion being 60%. GST would therefore be payable on 40% of the cost of the package to the purchaser, or $42. In this way, the proportionate amount of the operator's margin is also subject to tax.

Note that this exercise is normally needed only once — at the time the tour is costed out. However, should any of the original factors change (such as a rebate to the operator), the pro-ration exercise will have to be done again.

When tours are sold through a wholesale market (to retailers before being sold to consumers), the pro-rated percentage on which a retailer pays a wholesaler GST is to be the same percentage used on charges to consumers. Thus, if the wholesaler charges GST on 55% of the package, the retailer must charge GST on 55% of its price to consumers.

29. Interest and Penalties

Interest and penalties will be imposed on persons who, having the obligation or responsibility to do so, have failed to either pay or remit tax, or to pay instalments.

A prescribed rate of interest will be charged on late or deficient remittances or payments. It can be expected that this rate will be the same as that prescribed for income tax purposes. Both the interest and penalties will accrue on a daily compounded basis.

Persons failing to remit amounts required by the legislation will be faced with a 6% penalty per year, as well as interest at the prescribed rate. The penalty will be based on the amount that should have been paid.

For example, if a taxpayer has the liability to remit $10,000 of GST for sales for a period, failure to remit will result in charges of 6% on the $10,000 on a compounded basis.

For instalments, a similar rule will apply. A 6% penalty will be charged, in addition to interest. The penalty and interest will start from the time the instalment should have been paid to the earlier of the day on which the instalment (with accrued penalty and interest) is paid or the day on which tax on account of the instalment was payable is required to be remitted (keep in mind that instalments may represent the pre-payment of GST that is otherwise remitted at a later time).

Note that the amount of interest and penalties imposed on late or deficient instalments are payable only to the extent that they exceed the interest plus 6% paid on early or overpaid instalments.

When the date to remit tax has passed, the amount will be treated as an amount of net GST that has not been remitted and will continue to accrue interest and penalties.

Penalties and interest charges for late or deficient instalments will be reduced when Revenue Canada holds security for the payment or for any other reason under the legislation. In these circumstances, the 6% penalty will be applicable only when the total tax, net tax, instalments, penalty and interest (that have not been remitted) exceeds the value of the security.

Revenue Canada has the discretion to write off any penalties and interest charges when, added together, they do not exceed $25. Furthermore, the department has the authority to waive penalties and interest when payment of GST has been made after the person has complied with the conditions set out in a demand for payment from Revenue Canada.

The accrual of penalties will be suspended when Revenue Canada exercises its authority to extend the time for filing a return or providing any information for GST purposes. This suspension will not apply to interest, which will continue to accrue.

Revenue Canada has the authority to demand that a return be filed by any person, either for a particular period of time, or in relation to a particular transaction. Failure to comply will result in a penalty of the greater of $250 or 5% of the tax outstanding on the demand.

When a person has failed to provide documents or information to the department, a $100 penalty per occurrence may be imposed. This penalty can be waived by Revenue Canada, or where the person made an otherwise reasonable effort to comply.

Finally, a significant penalty will be imposed when a person makes a false statement or omission in a return or other document for a reporting period either knowingly or in circumstances amounting to gross negligence. The penalty in these situations will be equal to the greater of $250 or 25% of the amount in question.

IV. Real Estate

As a matter of public policy, the supply of residential housing and accommodation (with the exception of new housing) is exempted from GST (i.e., tax is not charged on the supply, but inputs cannot be recovered by the vendor). Conversely, the supply of real estate for commercial enterprises will generally be subject to tax in accordance with the general scheme of the legislation.

A variety of provisions are necessary to strike a balance between the inter-relationship of residential and commercial properties. For example, it is common practice to mix residential and commercial uses in a single complex. A series of mechanisms has been integrated into the GST system to deal with these issues. The object is to ensure that appropriate allocations for mixed-use property are made so that input credits can be claimed on that portion employed in commercial enterprises. Similarly, change-in-use rules have been established to ensure that the GST system does not subsidize residential housing through a circumvention of the input credit limitations on that type of supply.

Transitional rules and rebates are also used to make sure that existing real estate properties are integrated into the GST with a minimum of disruption or additional costs.

The impact of GST on real estate is relatively clear. Commercial real property that is fully taxable under GST will be available at reduced costs in relation to their cost under the federal sales tax system.

Federal sales tax charges represented a cost of construction and acquisition that was added to the purchase or lease price of property. Once removed, the true cost of commercial real property drops, since GST is not a cost, but a recoverable expense in an active business context.

At the same time, the cost of new housing will, in many cases, increase. Although federal sales tax charges for materials and other construction goods will be removed from the cost of a house, they normally represent a relatively small percentage of the finished product's purchase price.

GST on new housing will represent a 7% gross cost that is not recoverable by all home buyers. Some, who are eligible for new housing rebates, will recover a portion of the tax. Those who are not eligible will be subject to the full brunt of the GST.

Used housing will not be subject to GST on a gross cost basis, but will instead be exempted. This status means, however, that inputs incurred by vendors in relation to the used housing (such as GST paid for general upkeep and renovation) will continuously find their way into the price to a new purchaser. In some cases, the hidden inputs may exceed the tax burden associated with federal sales tax charges.

It is expected that residential markets will adjust downwards to accommodate the GST tax system.

1. Residential Real Estate: Buying and Selling

a. New Housing

Sales of new housing in Canada will be subject to GST in accordance with the normal scheme of the legislation. The tax will be equal to 7% of the cost of the residence.

Vendors will be entitled to claim input credits incurred to

construct new housing subject to GST in the ordinary manner.

New housing will, however, be subject to a rebate scheme designed to reimburse buyers of moderately priced housing for a portion of the GST cost. Government estimates show that the rebate is expected to reduce the impact of GST on qualifying new housing costs from 7% to an average of 4.5%. The rebates are available to individuals who purchase new housing from builders. For this purpose, builders are defined to include persons who buy unoccupied new houses for resale to the public.

Builders are also defined as persons who substantially renovate or convert existing properties into residential complexes. As a consequence of this rule, the rebates will be available for the purchase of renovated and converted properties as they would in the case of entirely new housing.

The rebate will apply to purchases of single-unit residential complexes as well as residential condominiums. Single-unit housing includes detached, semi-detached and row housing. Land immediately contiguous to the building that is reasonably necessary to its use and enjoyment as a residence for individuals (i.e., a yard and driveway) will be considered to be part of the residential complex for this purpose.

Rebates can be claimed when the acquisition from the builder is both for the land and building, conveyed in a single transaction. This may cause some difficulties for residents in areas where land cannot, as a matter of law, be conveyed to the owner of a residence.

For example, most of the land in Banff, Alberta, is owned by the federal government. Although residents are not entitled to buy the land, they can lease it on a long-term basis for residential purposes. It is likely that administrative concessions will have to be made in these situations in order to allow individuals in these unique positions to claim the rebate when the other conditions necessary to its availability are otherwise satisfied.

Rebates will not be available for investment properties or cottages. They may be claimed only for new housing that represents the purchaser's primary place of residence (unlike cottages or investment properties). Alternatively, the rebates will be available where the new housing is acquired as a primary place of residence for a relation of the purchaser. A person's relation is defined as any relative of the individual as defined for the purposes of the Income Tax Act, as well as a former spouse. Related persons are defined for income tax purposes to include individuals connected by blood relationship, marriage or adoption.

Only new housing with a total cost of less than $450,000 will qualify for rebate eligibility. When that cost exceeds this threshold, no rebates will be available for any part of the consideration paid for the housing. For this purpose, the total cost of a residential complex will include payment for properties or services that may reasonably be regarded as being incidental to the supply of the housing. For example, this might include built-in dishwashers and stoves, as well as free-standing garages and tool sheds.

The total cost will also include payments made for the supply of an interest in a particular unit. For example, this rule will apply to the acquisition of a condominium unit that is subsequently reassigned before occupation. Thus, should a unit be purchased from a builder for $250,000 and on assignment the final purchaser is required to pay an additional $35,000 to the assignor, the total cost for rebate purposes will be $285,000.

Note that rebates will be available only after all of the GST payable on the acquisition has been paid.

In ordinary circumstances, the rebate will be available when the housing is not occupied until after title has passed to the purchaser and construction is substantially complete. An exception is made for condominiums, where in practice purchasers (or their relations) often occupy the property before transfer of title on registration of the condominium complex (and in some cases before construction is completed on the entire residence).

Furthermore, the first occupant of the housing must be the purchaser or a relation. However, eligibility for the rebate may still be available if a purchaser sells the property before occupation as a used property that is exempt from GST. This might happen when unanticipated employment relocation forces a move and the sale of a new residence before the owner has moved in.

The rebate formula is designed to return approximately 2.5% of the 7% GST charged on a new housing sale when the total cost of the property is at or below $350,000. The rebate is proportionately phased out for housing priced between $350,000 and $450,000. As stated above, housing with a cost beyond the $450,000 threshold will not be entitled to any rebates.

For housing that costs $350,000 or less, the rebate will be equal to the lesser of $8,750 or 36% of the total GST paid by the claimant for the housing. For example, if housing costs are $350,000, a $24,500 GST liability will be imposed on the sale. That cost, multiplied by 36%, is equal to $8,820. Thus, the maximum rebate of $8,750 would be available in these circumstances.

If the housing had a cost of $250,000, a $17,500 GST liability would arise, 36% of which is $6,300 (which would represent the available rebate).

Housing with a cost between $350,000 and $450,000 will be subject to rebates determined in accordance with the following formula:

$$\$8{,}750 \times \frac{(\$450{,}000 - \text{A [total consideration for the house]})}{\$100{,}000}$$

For example, assume the total cost of housing was $400,000. Inserting this amount into the formula would result in the following rebate:

$$\$8{,}750 \times \frac{(\$450{,}000 - \$400{,}000)}{\$100{,}000} = \$8{,}750 \times .5 = \$4{,}375$$

On a $400,000 purchase price, $28,000 of GST would be payable. The rebate of $4,375 would therefore represent a recovery of only 15.625% of the GST component.

These examples illustrate the incentive that is inherent in the new housing rebate to acquire a residential complex at a cost that is at or slightly below the $350,000 threshold. In this way, the maximum rebate is available for GST purposes.

Subsequent additions and improvements may be subject to GST, but they will not reduce the rebate previously available on the initial acquisition. From a planning perspective, it may therefore be prudent to buy new housing that does not have all the appliances and finishing touches most buyers have looked for. This would help keep the cost down and maximize the rebate. The fixtures and added enhancements could then be purchased when the rebate has been received.

Individuals can apply for rebates up to four years from the date the new housing was acquired.

A special mechanism, established for this rebate, is designed to allow new home buyers to obtain benefits from the GST recovery with a minimum of delay. It is also designed to reduce administrative burdens associated with providing rebates to new home buyers. The mechanism allows vendors to either credit the rebate to a purchaser by paying the amount directly, or credit the rebate against GST owing on the purchase. The purchaser will have up to four years to apply for this credit from a vendor. This election will not preclude the purchaser from seeking the rebate directly from the government instead.

When this method is chosen, builders must forward the application for the rebate to Revenue Canada with their returns for the period in which the rebate was paid or credited to the purchaser. Interest will not apply to rebates that are so credited.

The GST remittance liability of the builder will accordingly be reduced by the rebate so paid or credited. This will provide builders with a marketing opportunity that they would be advised to use wherever possible.

b. Co-operative Housing

A rebate mechanism has been established for co-operative housing that is similar to that available for new housing. The threshold is slightly higher for co-operative housing, to reflect the GST paid on acquisition of the entire complex. The threshold of $481,500 is therefore considered to correspond to the $450,000 threshold for new housing.

Co-operative housing differs from conventional housing in that a purchaser normally acquires a "share" in the complex, entitling the purchaser to the use and occupation of a unit therein.

The conditions necessary to claim the rebate in these circumstances are virtually identical to those established for new housing.

c. Owner-Built New Housing

A special mechanism is also needed to provide rebates to owners who build their own housing. It is specifically available to individuals who either build or substantially renovate their primary residences, or hire another person (i.e., contractor or architect) to do so.

Under the self-supply rules (discussed below), owner-built houses will be subject to GST charges based on their fair market value. The rebates will be available to reduce this cost.

The rebates are virtually the same as those available for acquired (rather than owner-built) new housing, where the owner has paid GST for the cost of the land. Thus, 2.5% of the 7% GST paid for the property will be available as a rebate when its total cost is less than $350,000. The rebate is proportionately reduced when the cost is between $350,000 and $450,000 and is totally phased out at costs of more than $450,000.

When GST was not paid for the land on which the housing is built, the rebate will be reduced to reflect its tax-free nature.

Formal appraisals will be necessary when the value of the housing is close to or exceeds $350,000. They will not be necessary when the value is clearly below the $350,000 threshold. The rebate will be based on appraisals when they are considered necessary.

The first occupancy conditions applicable to owner-acquired new housing apply equally to owner-built housing.

Note that to claim a rebate, an owner will have up to two years from the earlier of the date the home is first occupied by the individual (or ownership is transferred to another individual before occupation) or the day construction or substantial renovation is completed.

In general terms, when an individual sells real property (excluding residential complexes, defined above), the sale will be exempt for GST purposes except when it is sold under one of the following conditions:

- The real property was used primarily in the course of a commercial activity.
- The real property was sold in the course of a commercial activity.
- An election has been made to treat the sale of property as taxable when it is sold as an "adventure in the nature of trade" (i.e., a one-time speculative investment for income, rather than capital gains, purpose). This election will be available only when the adventure in the nature of trade was not part of a commercial enterprise.
- As a consequence of the change-in-use rules, the person is deemed to have made a sale of the property in circumstances that give rise to a GST liability.

Thus, for example, this rule will govern the sale of vacation properties, hobby farms and land that is not used for business purposes. Sales of all of these properties will be exempt.

Note that farmland will be exempt on a sale to an individual that is related to the farmer (or a former spouse) as long as the property is subsequently used for the personal enjoyment of the individual. As well, tax will not be payable when a farmer converts a working property to a personal use property.

Sales of farmland developers or unrelated individuals will, however, be subject to tax in the ordinary course.

d. Used Housing

The supply of used housing is exempt from tax. Thus, individuals buying used housing will not have to pay GST on the cost of that property.

Since it is exempt, vendors selling used housing will not be entitled to claim input credits for the property. As a result, although GST will not represent a direct charge on the cost of used housing, it will be an indirect charge, reflected in the costs associated with the property that have been subject to non-recoverable GST charges.

These charges might relate to repairs and maintenance, as well as some municipal services, yard care and other services such as interior decorating or painting.

Costs relative to the acquisition of the property will also be subject to GST and result in an indirect tax on used housing purchases. This will include legal fees, title searches, building inspections and property surveys.

Where the used housing qualified as new housing at one point after January 1, 1991, it will have initially been subject to GST charges. It can be expected that the cost of the tax on the initial acquisition will be added to the cost of the house when it is subsequently sold as used housing. Used housing will not, however, be subject to rebates of any kind. The full 7% of GST will represent a cost to the purchaser.

Different tax consequences will arise when used residential housing is either converted to or from commercial uses. Special rules have been established to either impose GST liability or allow the recovery of inherent tax through notional input credits, depending on the circumstances. Refer to Chapter IV, "Commercial Real Estate," for more details.

e. Transitional Rules: Condominiums

It takes a long time to build and sell condominium projects. Many were in place and partially sold before the draft GST legislation was made public in October 1989.

If GST applied to those sales, a lot of developers and purchasers would be unfairly treated because of increased prices not originally taken into account.

To deal with this issue, special transitional rules have been established to except certain condominium sales from the system. GST will not be payable on residential condominiums bought by individuals under a written agreement that was executed before October 14, 1989, if possession and title will not be transferred until after 1990.

Similarly, unsold residential condominiums will be subject to the federal sales tax rebate that builders can collect for all unfinished units held at the time of GST implementation. Input credits may also be claimed on supplies acquired after 1990 for inclusion in the building.

A special 4% tax is, however, imposed on all of these "grandfathered" units. The object is to impose the same tax content on these sales as if federal sales tax and not GST had been imposed through the entire term of their construction.

f. Transitional Rules: Single Family Residential Housing

Similar transitional rules apply for single unit homes bought under written agreement entered into before October 14, 1989, if possession is not taken until after 1990. GST will not apply, but a 4% special tax will be payable.

The 4% tax is, however, payable on a sliding scale, unlike the tax on condominiums. The scale is as follows:

- If not more than 20% of the home is completed on January 1, 1991, the special tax will be 4% of the total consideration for the property.
- If more than 20% but not more than 60% of the home is completed on January 1, 1991, the special tax will be 2.5% of the total consideration for the property.
- If more than 60% but not more than 90% of the home is completed on January 1, 1991, the special tax will be 1% of the total consideration for the property.
- If the house was more than 90% complete on January 1, 1991, no special tax will be payable.

g. Real Estate Commissions

Real estate commissions will be subject to GST for both residential and commercial properties. They represent a service that is independent of the cost of property, whether new or used.

The fees cannot be recovered on the sale of housing. Accordingly, GST will give vendors an additional incentive to attempt the sale of housing without using agents.

2. Residential Real Estate: Leasing

Long-term residential rents and accommodation in boarding houses is exempt from the GST. Thus, tax will not be payable on those rents, and landlords will not be entitled to claim input credits incurred in relation to the supply.

Although the gross cost of residential rents escapes the full 7% tax burden, it is likely that inputs incurred by landlords will find their way into the cost of leasing. It is the only way these inputs can be recovered by the landlords.

It can be expected that market pressures and rent control legislation (in the provinces such as Ontario where it is well entrenched) will limit the ability of landlords to pass on their inputs by way of price increases in some circumstances.

The phrase "long-term rentals" is defined to include rental periods that are longer than one month. The rent must be paid for either a residential unit or complex. This will include houses and apartments, but will exclude motels, hotels and other similar accommodation, such as executive suites. As a result, long-term rentals of the latter category of accommodation will generally be subject to GST.

Note that short-term accommodation in rooming and boarding houses, or in other residential housing, will also be exempted from tax. In these circumstances, the rental charges must not exceed $20 per day or $140 per week.

Parking spaces, as long as they are incidental to the supply of exempt long-term accommodation, will also be exempt. This exemption is available whether or not the landlord charges separately for the space.

Note that the long-term rental exempt treatment will be extended to long-term rentals of land for mobile homes or other forms of residential units to be fixed on the land. Thus, space rentals in mobile home parks will be exempted. The space must be rented to an individual for a period exceeding one month.

This exemption will not apply to campground rentals or space rentals for motor homes and trailers. The exemption does not apply because they do not qualify as residential units or complexes. Thus, these charges will be subject to GST in the ordinary course.

Note that condominium fees charged for residential accommodation, whether to owners or lessees, will be exempt from GST. Thus, residential condominium corporations are in the same position vis-à-vis the GST as residential landlords — they cannot recover inputs directly. Again, it is likely that the inputs will find their way into the cost of the fees.

3. Commercial Real Estate

As noted above, commercial real estate transactions (including sales and leases) will be subject to GST. Thus, tax will be payable on the cost of commercial real estate and purchasers will be entitled to input tax credits. In that way, commercial purchasers or tenants will be able to recover the tax.

The general rule deals with the simple situations, though, involving wholly commercial transactions. There are a number of more complicated issues that have to be addressed for supplies that are only partially commercial. For the most part, these issues deal with the segregation of commercial use from residential use. This distinction is important because of entitlement to input credits.

If input credits are available for personal-use properties, or personal-use components of commercial properties, the GST system can, in many cases, effectively be subsidizing a supply that is otherwise exempt under the legislation.

There are a number of different situations in which this issue has to be addressed. Mixed-use properties, that is, those that combine the supply of commercial and residential property, are subject to rules that apportion entitlement to input credits between the two uses.

Similarly, when there has been a change in use, from commercial to residential, or vice versa, either an entitlement to recover previously limited credits or an obligation to repay previously claimed inputs will arise.

In some cases, individuals buying commercial real estate have to allocate between taxable and non-taxable uses differently than corporations. In other cases, where landlords build their own properties for rental in either commercial or residential settings (or both), GST might have to be paid as if they had purchased the buildings.

Ancillary issues, such as the treatment of condominium fees, real estate commissions, legal fees and costs of conveyance, as well as mortgage and insurance premiums, have to be considered in the context of whether they are subject to tax and whether the tax can be recovered as an input credit.

Finally, properties are improved, renovated, altered or converted, resulting in input taxes in addition to the tax that may have been payable on initial acquisition or construction. Determinations, based on personal versus commercial use, have to be made before these credits can be claimed.

If that wasn't enough, several transitional rules, applying to transactions straddling the GST start-up date, make the tax a factor that has to be faced even before the system starts.

The consequences of making mistakes can be costly. When a commercial enterprise cannot recover GST as an input credit, it will have to raise its prices to customers to accommodate the "cost" of the tax.

For example, in a mixed-use property, a landlord will recover

GST inputs in proportion to the percentage of commercial use in the property. For the residential part of the building, inputs have to be recovered indirectly by factoring the costs into rental rates.

If an allocation between the two uses is incorrect, causing the residential portion to be larger, a greater percentage of GST inputs on the commercial use will be lost. If the landlord has not factored the higher percentage of non-creditable credits into its residential rents, those inputs will not be recovered either directly or indirectly. That means they will reduce net profits to the landlord.

What can a mistake like that cost?

If annual inputs to a property are $500,000 and 40% are creditable (i.e., they can be claimed as credits and recovered in the system), the landlord has to factor the non-creditable inputs of $300,000 (or 60%) into residential rent rates.

If Revenue Canada is successful in allocating an additional 10% of the total inputsto the residential use, the landlord could lose $50,000 in non-creditable inputs. Since a re-allocation would happen on an audit and assessment that takes place long after rents for the period have been collected, the landlord would not be able to recover the additional non-creditable inputs of $50,000 by raising rents to tenants. Profits in the year the assessment was successful would therefore be reduced by $50,000. Similar problems can arise when mixed use property is sold. The moral of this example is that allocations have to be carefully considered and substantiated with facts. In this way, the potential for costly mistakes can be minimized.

The following commentaries consider the main issues in this area in more detail.

a. Mixed-Use Properties

It is commonplace to have mixed residential and commercial use properties. Examples are a strip mall with apartments on the second floor or a highrise apartment building, with retail stores on the ground level.

When the supply of real property includes a residential complex and other real property (i.e., commercial), the supply of the residential complex will be treated as a separate supply. Thus, if an apartment building with retail stores on the ground level is sold, this rule will treat the sale as if the apartment and retail portions of the property were separate buildings.

In this way, the rules that apply to residential complexes (see commentary under Residential Real Estate for more details) will apply to that part of the building separately from the rest.

Similarly, when an addition to a multiple-unit residential complex is made by a builder and the entire complex is sold, the sale of the previously existing part of the complex will be treated as an exempt supply. The sale of the addition will be treated as a separate property and the rules will apply accordingly. Thus, the addition may be taxable as a commercial property when the facts warrant that treatment.

When a mixed-use property is sold in a completely taxable transaction, the vendor will be able to recover input credits for GST not previously claimed on the non-commercial portion of the property. For example, a design firm sells a renovated house that was partially used (35%) as a residence by the president of the firm to another design group that will use the entire property in its operations. On the sale, the vendor can claim input credits against the non-commercial portion of the house. The amount claimed will be determined by multiplying the non-commercial portion of the property by the lesser of two amounts:

- The tax payable on the original purchase of the property by the vendor, as well as improvements, less any rebates available to the vendor, and
- The tax collected by the vendor on the sale of the property.

Thus, if the house was bought for $500,000 and was sold for $1 million, the inputs available on the sale would be equal to 35% x $35,000 (the lesser of the tax paid on acquisition and GST paid on disposition) = $12,500.

As a practical matter, vendors should keep this recovery in mind when negotiating the price of their properties. Excess returns from the GST system can provide room to reduce selling prices to accommodate quick sales.

b. Change in Use Rules: Registrants and Individuals

The first point to note is that these guidelines do not apply to individuals, who are dealt with under separate rules.

The rules are relevant to adjustments, either before or after the fact, of input credits.

In general terms, these rules apply to recapture previously claimed input credits where use in a commercial enterprise has been reduced from previous levels. The consequence will be a deemed disposition of the property, giving rise to a GST liability. In this way, previously claimed credits are recovered by the system.

The rules also apply to provide credits previously denied when an increase in commercial use has occurred.

This mechanism is necessary to prevent abuse of the system. If it were not in place, taxpayers could circumvent the limitations denying input credits for residential properties through commercial acquisitions that were later converted to non-commercial uses.

The mechanism is also necessary to prevent double taxation when previously non-creditable exempt acquisitions were made and subsequent taxable transactions occur, resulting in tax being payable on property for which inputs have not been recovered.

When the commercial use of a capital real property is decreased, the owner (registrant) will be treated as having sold that part of the property that is in proportion to the decrease in use. Tax will be deemed to have been collected, equal to the lesser of two amounts:

- GST that would have been paid had that proportion of the property been sold at its fair market value at the time, and
- The tax that was previously paid on that portion.

Assume that a building bought for $2 million is used 30% for commercial purposes and 70% for residential purposes on the date of acquisition. This would result in GST to the purchaser of $42,000 (i.e., $2 million x 30% x 7%) that is claimed as an input credit. After acquisition, the owner reduces commercial use by 15%. A disposition of 15% of the building would be deemed to occur, resulting in proceeds of $300,000 (i.e., $2 million x 15%) that would be subject to GST at 7% for a tax liability of $21,000. The $21,000 tax payment would represent the recapture of 50% of the input credits claimed on acquisition of the building, before its commercial use was reduced by half. Thus, a portion of the original inputs that related to taxable activities is returned to the system.

Different rules apply when the change in commercial use to personal use exceeds the 90% "exclusive" threshold. In these circumstances, an allocation between commercial and personal use for the purposes of input credit claims is not allowed. Rather, input credits are no longer allowed on the property.

When personal use exceeds 90%, the owner will be deemed to have sold the property for fair market proceeds. When the property was exclusively used for commercial purposes before the change (i.e., a working condominium is converted to a personal residence), GST will be payable on its full fair market value.

However, when the property was previously mixed use between commercial and personal (or other category), tax will have to be paid only on the portion that related to commercial. A $1-million building, previously used 40% as a studio and 60% as a residence, would, on conversion, give rise to GST of 40% x $1 million x 7% = $28,000.

Note that this represents the effect of several rules working in conjunction. On a change of use, a disposition of the entire property is deemed to take place, with tax payable on the lesser of the total tax that was previously payable on the property (including improvements) and that tax that would be payable had it been sold at fair market value. Input credits are then available for the deemed disposition, resulting in GST liability only on the commercial portion of the property as it stood before the change in use.

On the other side of the issue, when property that was not used for commercial purposes at all (or was converted to exclusive non-commercial uses) is subsequently used for commercial enterprises, a notional input credit will be available to allow the owner to extract inherent GST. Note that this treatment will not be available to property that is exempt (i.e., such as a residential house) with no inherent GST burden.

The rule is designed to allow a full input credit when the property will be used exclusively in commercial enterprises. When not used exclusively, a proportionate input credit claim will be available in proportion to the commercial use.

In specific terms, a registrant in these situations will be considered to have paid GST on the change in use equal to the lesser of two amounts:

- The total tax originally paid or payable on the acquisition of the property, plus tax paid on subsequent improvements, less rebates recovered (available in some cases), and
- The GST that would be payable had the property been acquired for its fair market value at the time the change began.

For example, dentists operating their practice out of a townhouse, in which the basement suite is commercially rented, move to larger premises and rent the entire townhouse property to an architectural firm. The property is worth $1 million, and previously, only 10% related to the commercial rent, with the balance relating to exempt dental services. At the time the building was purchased, full GST of $56,000 was paid on an $800,000 purchase price.

Notional tax paid on the townhouse would equal the lesser of $56,000 (the total tax paid on acquisition) and $70,000 (the GST that would have been paid on a fair market value disposition). In this way, the original $56,000 paid as GST would be recoverable as an input credit.

Similar rules apply when there has been an increase in commercial uses, below the exclusive threshold (i.e., 90%). In these circumstances, notional tax will be considered to have been paid for the disposition of that portion of the property that has been converted to commercial uses. The notional tax can then be recovered as an input credit.

The formula for determining the notional GST in these situations is somewhat different from that provided above. Here, the percentage increase in commercial use, based on the total use of the real property, will be multiplied by the lesser of two amounts:

- The tax that would have been payable on the acquisition of the property (had it not been exempted, or had it been the subject of an election on the transfer of a business as a going concern), as well as rebates the owner was entitled to and the tax that would have been payable on subsequent improvements, and
- The tax that would have been payable had the property been acquired for its fair market value at that time.

A separate set of rules has been established for individuals who directly acquire capital real property for commercial uses. These rules deal with input credits on acquisition, as well as changes in use (whether increases or decreases in commercial use) and the treatment of improvements.

As a general proposition, individuals will be entitled to claim full input credits on the acquisition of capital real property that is "primarily" (i.e., more than 50%) used in commercial enterprises. When the commercial use is more than 50% but less than the 90% "exclusive" threshold, an allocation may be made between commercial and non-commercial uses for input credit purposes. When the commercial use is less than the 50% threshold, no apportionment of credits is available.

Similarly, when a change of personal-use property to commercial exceeds the 50% threshold, notional input credits will be available in proportion to the change in commercial use. The credits will be determined by much the same formulas noted above for non-individual owners that experience an increase in commercial uses.

When property primarily (more than 50%) used for commercial purposes is the subject of a change in use that increases the commercial component, a notional input credit will be available in proportion to the commercial use increase. Again, the formulas are similar to those noted above for properties owned by registrants other than individuals. Note that notional inputs will be available only if the individual has registered for GST purposes.

If an individual makes an improvement to the property, input credits will be available for that cost only when it is used primarily for commercial purposes. When it is used primarily for personal enjoyment, credits will be restricted.

c. Conversions to Personal or Residential Use

GST will be payable when an individual appropriates his or her commercial-use real property for personal use or the use of a related individual or former spouse (except where the property was a residential complex). The individual is deemed to have sold the property at the time the property is appropriated.

GST will have to be remitted for the reporting period in which the conversion occurred, based on the fair market value of that property. The object is to treat the conversion as if the individual had bought the property from someone else in a taxable transaction. This rule doesn't apply to residential complexes because the individual could have otherwise acquired that type of property exempt from tax.

Other rules apply when a person converts commercial real property into a residential complex without substantially renovating the complex ("substantial renovation" is discussed in more detail under the Self-Supply section below). In these circumstances, the person will be treated as a builder that substantially renovated the property as a residential complex.

This treatment is designed to have a number of effects. If the person buys used business properties and converts them to residential complexes for resale, the system will apply tax in the same manner that it is applied to a builder selling new residential complexes. If the person is an individual that intends to use the property as a primary home, housing rebates will be available, if the individual is eligible.

Alternatively, if the person is an individual who converts a building used in a business to a personal residence, resulting in tax paid on the change in use, the individual will also be treated as having substantially renovated the complex and may be entitled to rebates for owner-built homes (see "Residential Real Estate" discussed earlier in this chapter for more details on these rebates).

d. Self-Supply of Real Estate

Landlords often build or renovate their own residential properties for subsequent rental to tenants. Since this supply is exempt, it is necessary to impose notional tax liabilities to treat the landlord as if it had purchased the property in the marketplace for rental purposes.

A number of different rules apply, depending on the type of complex involved and the nature of the self-supply (i.e., renovation, alteration or construction).

The term "substantial renovation" is important to this area. When a building has been substantially renovated and forms part of (or is) a residential complex after the renovation, it will be treated as a new complex for tax purposes.

A building is substantially renovated when substantially all of the building, excluding the foundation, exterior walls, interior supporting walls, staircases, floors and roof, has been renovated, removed or replaced.

When a builder either constructs or substantially renovates a residential complex that is thereafter rented to residential tenants, or is occupied by the builder as a residence, the property will be deemed to have been sold and repurchased by the builder.

The result is that the builder is required to remit GST on the fair market value of the complex for the earlier of the reporting period in which the complex has been completed, or is rented out.

The effect of this rule is to tax that portion of the value added to the complex by the builder. Subsequent sales may be exempted if tax has been paid under this rule.

Note that this rule will not apply when the builder is an individual who uses the property as a primary home, to the extent input credits have not been claimed on either the acquisition of the land, construction or renovation.

Other exclusions to this self-supply rule include universities, school authorities and public colleges building student residences, and registrants constructing residences at remote work sites.

In some situations, the builder of a substantially completed residential condominium complex has allowed the purchaser possession of a unit under agreement before the entire complex has been registered. The purchaser either occupies the unit or rents it out and the agreement is terminated (except when termination arises from non-performance) without execution of a new agreement. In these circumstances, the builder will have to pay GST on the fair market value of the unit at the time the agreement is terminated.

Landlords who self-supply a substantially completed multiple unit residential complex, such as an apartment building, will be considered to have made a taxable supply of the entire complex on the day the first unit is rented out or it is occupied by the builder (to the extent the builder is an individual). However, when units are rented out before substantial completion of the complex, this rule will apply at the time of substantial completion.

When an addition is made to an existing residential complex, such as a new level in an apartment building, the self-supply rules will apply at the later of the time the addition is first occupied or upon substantial completion. GST will be payable on the fair market value of the addition at that time.

Note that even when a residential complex or addition thereto is not substantially completed, it will be considered to be substantially completed when more than 90% of the residential units are occupied after the construction or renovation began.

In some cases, renovations or alterations to real estate will not qualify as substantial renovations. In these circumstances, the builder will effectively be required to remit GST on the labour costs involved in renovating the property. GST would not, however, be imposed on costs that were already subject to GST, such as materials and sub-contracted services.

This rule provides that the person is considered to have made a taxable supply for value equal to the total of all non-taxable costs that can be attributed to the renovation (other than financing or the original cost) that would be included in determining the property's adjusted cost base for the purposes of the Income Tax Act, where the property was a capital property of the taxpayer.

This supply will be treated as having been made either at the time the renovation is substantially completed, or the time ownership of the complex is transferred, whichever is earlier. Further, the person is deemed to have collected GST on the supply determined on the total of all such costs.

Note that this rules applies strictly to renovation costs and not to usual maintenance and repair costs that would not otherwise be recognized as part of the property's capital cost for income tax purposes.

e. Leasing Commercial Real Estate

The provision of leased commercial property will be subject to GST as a supply. Thus, lease payments or liabilities will give rise to tax.

By implication, when property is leased in commercial circumstances, the recipient of the supply will normally be entitled to recover taxes paid on the lease as an input credit. In some cases, however, recipients will not be using the premises for taxable activities (such as dentists providing health services) and they will not be able to recover the tax.

Note that the liability to remit GST will be on the landlord. The liability will arise at the earlier of the time the payments were due under the lease agreement, or the time they were actually paid. As a consequence, landlords will find themselves financing the cost of GST remittances for tenants who do not pay rent on time.

GST will be payable on lease payments regardless of how they are determined. Thus, it will apply on such charges as percentage rent, where landlords (such as in retail leasing situations) recover a percentage of a tenant's sales in addition to a flat-rate rental charge. It should also include the cost of any operating charges (excluding GST paid to acquire them) that is incurred by the landlord and passed through to a tenant as part of the leasing cost.

Care will have to be taken when allocations must be made between rentals of mixed-use properties. It is important to ensure that common area allocations with respect to inputs are reasonably made to avoid subsequent assessments that result in reduced credit claims that cannot be recovered from residential tenants.

f. Miscellaneous Costs

Real estate transactions carry with them a number of ancillary costs that will be subject to GST. They include real estate commissions, legal fees, title search and transfer fees.

Fees associated with financing, including mortgage brokerage, placement and commitment fees, will be exempted as financial services and will not be subject to GST. Mortgage and insurance premiums will also be exempted as financial services.

4. Contractors and Developers

The rules relating to the imposition of GST on real estate transactions, outlined in the preceding three sections on this topic, are important to contractors. They determine how much tax must be paid and when it has to be remitted.

Contractors and developers must, however, also focus on how GST is to be treated contractually. Industry practices have, to now, been based on a system that has different consequences than the GST. As a result, these practices will have to be changed to accommodate the different effects of the tax.

As noted earlier, the GST regime and the federal sales tax system are fundamentally different in relation to the construction industry. Federal sales tax is currently regarded as a cost of providing goods under a construction contract.

GST, on the other hand, will normally not represent a cost of providing either goods or services. Taxable registrants will be entitled to recover any GST that has been incurred to purchase goods or services, either as a direct refund or as an input tax credit that reduces the amount of GST collected on sales that must be remitted to the federal government.

Contractors will be entitled to recover the cost of providing construction services and goods as input credits on all of the buildings they work on. It doesn't matter whether the construction is residential or commercial.

For example, assume that a contractor purchases $100,000 of conduit, paying $7,000 in GST at the time of delivery. The contractor will be entitled to recover the $7,000 in one of two ways:

1. If the contractor has collected GST on its sales for the accounting period in question, it will be able to offset the $7,000 input credit against the GST it has collected in that period and remit the balance to the federal government, or
2. If the contractor has not collected GST on its sales for the accounting period in question, it will be entitled to apply for a $7,000 GST refund directly from the federal government.

Most builders and developers will be in an equivalent position. GST charged by contractors on services and the materials they provide will represent an input tax credit that will be fully recoverable.

Some owners, such as universities and hospitals, will be entitled to GST recovery by way of a special rebate system, as opposed to the ordinary input tax credit system.

In this regard, it should be noted that municipalities, universities, schools and hospitals (commonly known as the "MUSH" sector) will be exempt under the GST system. As a result, although they will not charge tax on their sales, they will also not be entitled to recover their input taxes as a direct credit. Rather, the government will implement a special rebate mechanism that will be designed to compensate these entities for the cost of GST on their purchases. It is not expected that the rebates will be equal to 100% of their inputs. As a consequence, these entities will likely be more resistant to GST charges than taxable owners who will directly recover all GST incurred on construction projects.

Depending on the circumstances, contractors will have an obligation to collect and remit GST for their supply. They will be faced with new compliance burdens that have not previously been part of the industry. This could present a hardship for the sub-trades, where small operations and sole proprietorships are common. The Quick Accounting Method (discussed in Chapter III) could, however, solve many of these compliance problems.

As a general rule, most registered taxpayers (with the exception perhaps of retailers) should identify GST as an "extra" amount over and above the contract price. This will simplify accounting and ensure that all parties to a contract can clearly identify the net contract price. Each party can then easily assess the GST impact on its particular circumstances, and contracts can be standardized regardless of the ability of a purchaser to obtain a rebate of the entire GST.

The construction industry has, for many years, relied on industry standard contracts to govern its relationships with owners. It will be critical that these agreements be varied to accommodate the GST and remove the obsolete language that relates to the federal sales tax system.

Though GST will be legally payable on each and every commercial transaction after implementation, parties to an agreement can determine whether the tax will be calculated as an extra amount on the contract price, or whether it will be included in the contract price. It will generally be easier to calculate GST as an extra amount in addition to the contract price.

Since most parties to a construction contract will recover the GST, a contract price that excludes GST should represent a true net price in all circumstances.

It will be important to ensure that not only is an owner obligated to pay GST as an additional amount in relation to the contract price, but that GST payments are made with each progress billing and cash allowance. This will provide contractors with the funds they are required to remit to the federal government in relation to each payment, providing their receivables are maintained on a current basis.

In the absence of an obligation on an owner to pay GST on each payment (as opposed to delaying until the final payment of the contract price), contractors could find themselves financing the cost of GST remittances until they can be recovered from an owner at the completion of a project.

Special rules have been established to deal with the imposition of GST on construction industry holdbacks. Generally, holdbacks will not become subject to GST until the earlier of the day the holdback is paid, or it becomes payable. This rule will apply to holdbacks that are established by way of legislation (either federal or provincial) or pursuant to written real estate construction agreements.

Provincial sales tax ("PST") is similar to federal sales tax in that it represents a cost of providing materials for a construction project. It will continue to represent a cost after GST is implemented.

It will be important to determine whether PST should be

included in the contract price , or whether it is an extra amount over and above the contract price. At present, it is included in the contract price pursuant to industry standard agreements in order to be consistent with the treatment of federal sales tax. It will probably be best to continue to include the cost of PST in the contract price for accounting purposes under GST. This will simplify proposals for accounting purposes and will not conflict with the treatment of GST, which is not a cost, but a recoverable expense.

The federal sales tax system continues in force until midnight, December 31, 1990. It will therefore be necessary to retain the contractual clauses contained in the present industry standard agreements and ensure that they remain in full force and effect until all claims are satisfied with respect to the federal sales tax regime in accordance with the obligations imposed by the agreements.

Thus, for example, should a federal sales tax rebate to an institution such as a university or hospital be disputed and remain unresolved for several years after GST implementation, the pre-1991 agreements regarding entitlement and security interests in relation to that disputed rebate must remain in force and effect until the matter is concluded.

When the GST was first proposed, federal sales tax inventory refunds were an important part of the scheme. Without them, the new system would result in rampant double taxation.

A main problem of moving from the old system to the new is making sure that manufactured goods are not subject to both systems of taxation. By providing taxpayers with a federal sales tax rebate for inventories owned on January 1, 1991, products will not be subjected to both levels of taxation. Rather, the federal sales tax will theoretically be flushed out of the cost of inventory and recovered by inventory owners.

For these purposes, inventory is generally defined to include goods described in the taxpayer's inventory that are held for sale, lease or rental to others in the ordinary course of business. A special rule has been designed specifically for building materials. Under this rule, an inventory refund will be available for the materials held for use by a taxpayer in the construction or renovation of a building or structure as long as they have not been incorporated into the structure and have not been delivered to the job site. Furthermore, these inventories must not be included in the description of another taxpayer's inventory.

The December 19, 1989, Notice of Ways and Means Motion on GST proposed that several standardized "rebate percentages" will be available to all taxpayers claiming the inventory refund, thereby providing equal treatment under the scheme.

A special rebate percentage of 5.6% has been proposed for construction material. The exact method of determining the rebate is not yet available and a number of factors may be included in the formula. However, it is expected at this time that taxpayers will be given a refund equal to an "inventory value" that is multiplied by the applicable rebate percentage.

Two reasons are put forward for this global approach. First, the government asserts that tax-extra invoicing is often an inaccurate measure of actual federal sales tax content, given that adjustments, deductions and allowances available to licensed manufacturers are usually not reflected. Second, the government claims that differentiating firms by industry and providing different trade level rebate percentages would be impractical. As a consequence, all contractors will be entitled to federal sales tax refunds for qualifying inventories held on January 1, 1991.

A number of other transitional provisions will be enacted with the main GST legislation to govern pre-payments in 1990 for the supply of goods and services in 1991. Several special provisions have been established for contracts that involve progress payment and that will be particularly applicable to contractors.

These transitional provisions essentially provide that no GST will be payable on progress payments and any holdbacks to the extent that the payments and holdbacks relate to property delivered or services performed before 1991. Alternatively, when the payments and holdbacks are attributable to property delivered or services performed after 1990, GST will be payable on those amounts, except when the supplier is not a registrant.

By implication, where a progress payment and holdback relates to the delivery of goods or services both during 1990 and 1991, a reasonable apportionment will have to be made and GST applied to the post-1990 goods and services portion of the payment or holdback.

Contractors and developers will have to take all of these factors into account when negotiating contractual relationships in relation to their real estate supply.

V. Transition: From Federal Sales Tax to GST

New tax systems cannot be implemented in a vacuum. Transitional rules are critical to limit double taxation (i.e., that arises by imposing GST on federal sales taxes inherent in goods) and to apply the tax fairly to transactions that were partially completed prior to the effective date of the new system.

Basically, GST should not be paid for goods or services provided before 1991. Alternatively, it should be paid on supplies made after 1990.

There are a number of different issues addressed by the GST transitional rules. Many of them deal with situations in which goods or services supplied in 1991 are paid for in 1990. Others deal with the payment in 1991 for goods or services delivered in 1990.

The rules attempt to stop taxpayers from circumventing GST by pre-paying for 1991 supplies. They also operate to limit the application of GST on supplies made prior to the 1991 implementation date.

The transitional rules can be divided into several categories.

1. Pre-1991 Contracts and Agreements

The GST applies to contracts entered into prior to January 1, 1991. In some cases, the obligation to collect GST exists for payments made after August 31, 1989 (discussed in detail below). Taxpayers will be in for big surprises if that hasn't been kept in mind when negotiating contracts that straddle the GST implementation date.

In general, the GST will apply to all contracts that exist at its effective date, without regard to possible consequences.

A variety of special provisions will, however, be established to override the general application of the GST and address the transition from the present system. Some of the main provisions include:

- When title to goods presently subject to federal sales tax (i.e., sold by a manufacturer or wholesaler) is transferred, or the goods are actually delivered prior to 1991, GST will not apply. If neither delivery nor title transfer occurs prior to that time, GST will apply. In this way, only federal sales tax or GST will apply to the goods, not both.
- Invoices issued prior to 1991 for goods and services supplied after 1990 will not limit the application of GST. Thus, taxpayers will have to do more than merely issue invoices to avoid GST on goods and services arranged prior to the implementation date (i.e., such as transfer title).
- When non-federal sales tax goods are delivered or title is passed prior to 1991, no GST will be applied as long as an invoice is issued or payments are made before March 1, 1991. The same applies to services, as long as they are performed prior to 1991. Thus, when invoices are issued after March 1, GST will apply even though the supply occurred prior to the implementation date. This exception will not apply, however, to lease payments for real property or chattel rentals, or partial payments on construction-in-progress.

Several general rules apply when payments are made before 1991 for goods to be delivered, or services to be performed, after 1990.

- Payments made by corporations, partnerships and sole proprietorships between September 1, 1989, and August 31, 1990, will be subject to GST. Purchasers will be liable to pay the tax on a self-assessment basis. They will have the obligation to file a return by April 1, 1991, remitting the tax that was payable for the supply. Special rules are, however, established for continuous supplies (such as electricity and cable television — discussed below).
- Vendors will be liable to collect GST on payments made after August 31, 1990, and before January 1, 1991. Tax will have to be collected only on that part of the payment that relates to the goods or services to be delivered after 1990. (Note that this rule will not apply to prepaid newspaper and periodical subscriptions — discussed below).

Budget arrangements will not be subject to these rules. Rather, GST will be payable only on amounts invoiced after 1991. However, a special year-end calculation-reconciliation has to be made that results in GST being payable on supplies made after 1990. Registrants will be obligated to make this reconciliation before 1992 in order to use this special rule with respect to budget arrangements. Otherwise, the ordinary pro-ration rules will apply.

These rules are introduced to limit the ability of taxpayers to circumvent the application of GST through long-term contracts. Although these precautions are necessary, they carry great potential for serious problems, particularly for taxpayers who do not know or refuse to take account of their application to pre-1991 payments.

Take the last set of rules. They impose an obligation on both vendors and purchasers to account for GST on transactions occurring prior to 1991, including some pre-payments that have already taken place. If GST is not accounted for, someone could be out of pocket.

For example, assume that a group of architects collects $1,000,000 on June 1, 1990, in pre-payment of services to be provided for architectural drawings to be delivered in 1991. If the group, as vendor, does not collect an additional $70,000 for the GST liability, the GST payment will come out of the $1 million pre-payment. At the same time, the purchaser will be entitled to recover the $70,000 paid by the group after 1991. This will have the practical effect of reducing the contract price by $70,000.

Similarly, many existing agreements provide that the total contract price will include any taxes imposed by the federal government. In these situations, GST will be taken out of the gross contract price. Since purchasers will be allowed to recover the new GST component, total contract prices will be reduced by the taxes paid, as in the example above.

Fixed-price contracts and long-term leases are most susceptible to transitional problems under the GST. The real issues will relate to tax clauses in those agreements.

Depending on the method used in an agreement to determine contract prices, the imposition of GST may or may not be an issue. When a contract stipulates that taxes associated with the transaction are an item to be added to the agreed price, GST will normally not represent an additional cost, on the basis that a taxable purchaser will incur the liability and recover it fully as an input tax credit.

However, when an agreement stipulates that the contract price includes all taxes, GST will effectively reduce the net return to a vendor. This will occur because the purchaser will be in a position to recover the GST component of a fixed price agreement regardless of whether it was an additional component in the transaction.

For example, assume that an agreement provides for a contract price of $1,000,000, exclusive of any taxes, to be paid after 1990. In these circumstances, the price would be grossed up to the purchaser by the GST component (expected to be $70,000 at the proposed 7% rate) and would be directly recovered by that party as an input tax credit.

When the contract price was $1,000,000 "inclusive" of GST, though, the price would not be grossed up to the purchaser by the GST component. Rather, the vendor would be obligated contractually to remit GST on the basis that the $1,000,000 was a tax-included price.

At the same time, the purchaser would remain entitled to recover the GST remitted by the vendor (approximately $65,420) as an input credit. This would result in a net return of $934,580 to the vendor under a fixed price contract that contained a tax-inclusive clause, as compared to one that contained a tax-exclusive clause.

It is clear that vendors under fixed-price contracts that straddle the GST implementation date stand to have their net returns reduced by 7% as a consequence of the introduction of this system.

Some purchasers, on the other hand, will not be receptive to having GST added to the price of a long-term, fixed-price contract. Exempt purchasers are not in a position to recover GST inputs, except by raising prices to their customers. Consumers also cannot recover GST paid on their purchases.

In both cases, adding GST to the cost of a contract will not merely represent a cash-flow adjustment (i.e., taxable purchasers pay GST for goods and services but get the tax back eventually). Rather, it will mean that the price of the supply has gone up by 7%.

This can cause enormous difficulties for exempt purchasers, that may not have budgets that can accommodate a 7% overrun on the cost of a project. With the severe constraints on educational and health-care funding, it can be expected that universities and hospitals will find it difficult to renegotiate fixed-price contracts that increase costs by 7% (in spite of rebates that may ultimately be recovered).

As many organizations are both vendor and purchaser, they will be prudent to address this issue after an analysis of their fixed-price contracts and perhaps instigate negotiations to resolve potential conflicts. It is also important for entities in these circumstances to develop guidelines for contracts currently under negotiation to ensure that GST is adequately addressed.

These rules will provide all businesses with incentives to start reviewing agreements to insure that they do not lose as a consequence of the transitional rules. It can be expected that contract renegotiations to accommodate GST will become a common occurrence.

2. Goods and Services Provided in 1990

Goods and services are often provided in the marketplace before payment. For example, accountants provide tax advice in December but don't invoice a client until the first quarter of the new year.

As a general rule, when goods or services are provided in 1990, GST will not be payable. However, for the rule to apply, invoices for pre-1991 supplymust be issued before May 1, 1991. If not, GST will be payable on the 1990 supply.

Businesses and consumers can expect that this will cause a flurry of invoices to be issued before the end of April, 1991, for all goods and services supplied in 1990. It will probably be in the best interests of most purchasers to ensure that invoices are issued before the deadline in order to avoid extra GST charges where they shouldn't apply.

3. Continuous Supplies

Many goods and services are supplied on a continuous basis — electricity, heat, water, lights and the like. Rules have been established to pro-rate these supplies between those provided in 1990 and those provided in 1991.

Basically, GST will apply only to supplies made after 1990 and not to those provided before 1991. However, continuous supplies obtained in 1990 will avoid tax liability only when they are invoiced before May 1, 1991.

4. Federal Sales Tax Inventory Rebate

The federal sales tax inventory rebate that will be available once the GST becomes law in 1991 may not be all it was thought to be, now that actual tax contents will not be refunded.

The Department of Finance has chosen, instead, to apply several generic rebate percentages to every business in Canada. The unavoidable result: full federal sales tax refunds will not be made.

When the GST was first proposed, federal sales tax inventory refunds were an important part of the scheme. Without them, the new system would result in rampant double taxation.

Avoiding double taxation is an unwritten rule that the Department of Finance has rarely, if ever, broken. Revenue Canada is quick to relieve double taxation when it is found.

As stated before, the two systems of commodity taxation are fundamentally different. Federal sales tax is currently regarded as a cost of providing goods under a contract. It is a one-time charge that is generally added on to a manufacturer's selling price and is never recovered, except by special-purpose purchasers, such as universities and hospitals.

GST, on the other hand, will normally not represent a cost of providing either goods or services. It will apply to each and every commercial transaction, up to and including consumer sales. Most enterprises will recover all GST incurred to purchase goods or services, either as a direct refund or as an input tax credit. In turn, the amount of GST collected on sales that must be remitted to the federal government will be reduced.

The biggest problem of moving from the old system to the new is making sure that manufactured goods are not subject to both systems of taxation, a nearly impossible feat in practical terms.

The most obvious solution turned out to be the best answer. By providing taxpayers with a federal sales tax rebate on inventories owned on January 1, 1991, the main goal could be reached — only goods subject to GST on sales after 1990 would be subject to the new regime, the old tax having been flushed out by way of refund.

As with all sound theories, practicalities got in the way. How were businesses to determine, with any accuracy, the federal sales tax content of their inventories?

In the past, formulas have been used to estimate federal sales tax content when actual figures were unavailable. The problem with these formulas is that they often identify as little as only two-thirds of true federal sales tax content.

The original GST proposals suggested that similar formulas would be used to determine federal sales tax content for purposes of the one-time inventory rebate. As an alternative, however, actual tax would be rebated where it could be determined with any accuracy.

This alternative (i.e., rebating actual tax contents) was supposed to provide taxpayers, particularly large retailers that purchase directly from manufacturers, with increased entitlements to the federal sales tax rebate by having their suppliers identify the tax as a separate item on invoices during 1990.

In that way, actual federal sales tax content could be more accurately estimated, providing the maximum possible assurance that goods sold after 1990 would be subject to little, if any, double taxation.

The December 19, 1989 Notice of Ways and Means Motion on GST put an end to that type of planning. In it, the government stated that it would impose standardized "rebate percentages" to all taxpayers claiming the inventory refund, thereby treating all equally under the scheme.

Two reasons were put forward for this global approach. First, the government asserted that tax extra invoicing is often an inaccurate measure of actual federal sales tax content, given that adjustments, deductions and allowances available to licensed manufacturers are usually not reflected. Second, the government claimed that differentiating firms by industry and providing different trade level rebate percentages would be impractical.

Although this global approach is somewhat attractive from an administrative perspective, it is doubtful that it will provide as high an inventory refund as the tax-extra invoicing approach in many instances.

Retailers should be the biggest winners under the planned manufacturer's sales tax rebate percentages announced by Finance Minister Michael Wilson on June 1, 1990.

Seven different rebate factors have been announced. The general rebate factor, which applies to most inventories, has been set at 8.1%. The others include:

- 5.6% for building materials;
- 2.8% for mobile homes and modular building units;
- 2.5% for small grocery and convenience stores;
- 11.1% for motor vehicles;
- 1.4% for propane; and
- actual per litre manufacturer's sales tax applied on December 31, 1990.

The practical implications of these rebates are clear. When the content of a particular inventory is relatively low in comparison to its overall cost, then the rebate factors, particularly the 8.1%, will go a long way towards rebating all (and perhaps in some cases more) than the inherent manufacturer's tax. Conversely, when tax content is high, a healthy portion (as much as 5.4% in some cases) will not be recovered.

Retailers will normally have the lowest tax content in their inventories and can expect the rebates to represent a healthy return. It may therefore be in the best interests of many retailers to build up large inventories prior to year end in order to maximize the effect of the rebate. If they delay purchasing inventory immediately after implementation, suppliers may not pass on the full tax savings (which may represent lower returns to the suppliers in any event, resulting in reduced potential savings for everyone).

Wholesalers with high tax content inventories delay purchases from manufacturers under GST. They should experience greater savings by waiting and buying goods free of the 13.5% manufacturer's tax (in return for a 7% charge that can be recovered) than they would with the rebate.

Grocery stores will be able to save time and money by using the special 2.5% rebate factor on all their tax paid and tax-exempt inventories. In this way, they won't have to try to segregate between the different goods, a difficult exercise at the best of times.

Making rebate percentages public now should also result in tangible benefits to consumers. By estimating tax rebates in the last two quarters of 1991, vendors might be able to adjust pricing variables in order to pass on savings to customers in the first and second quarters of 1991.

5. Residential Condominiums

See Chapter IV, Section 1, "Residential Real Estate," for details.

6. Memberships

Memberships are treated as the supply of services. The right to acquire a membership (such as a share in a golf club) is not treated as a supply of services. Therefore, memberships are subject to the same transitional rules established for services, noted above (i.e., tax is payable for the supply after 1990 and not for supply provided prior to 1991 if invoiced by May 1991).

Lifetime memberships are treated differently. If a lifetime membership is partially or totally paid after August 1990 and before 1991, the amount of the payment that exceeds 25% of the total cost of the membership will be subject to tax. In effect, when lifetime memberships are bought after August 1990, 75% of the cost will be subject to GST, whether paid before or after the January 1, 1991, implementation date.

7. Magazine Subscriptions

After 1990 all magazine subscriptions will be subject to GST. As a concession to the industry, subscriptions that are pre-paid before 1991 will not be subject to GST in spite of the fact that the payment relates to the supply of goods after implementation.

This rule has been established to avoid the compliance nightmare that would be created if apportionments were to be made in respect of these prescriptions. It would be virtually impossible to determine, with any accuracy, how much GST should be payable for a particular subscription until after an order was placed.

8. Leases: Tangible Personal Property

A special relieving rule has been established for long-term tangible personal property leases, such as equipment. Leases executed before August 8, 1989, will not be subject to GST. This rule applies to conventional leases and leases with buy-out clauses.

Thus, at the end of a lease that is grandfathered under this rule, the equipment can be purchased free of GST.

GST will also not be payable in 1991, 1992 or 1993 on leases for automobiles or equipment used by medical and other health-care practitioners. This rule will apply only if possession of the property is transferred before 1991. GST will not be payable if the lease payments represent either rent for periods prior to 1994 or a purchase option for the buy-out of the equipment.

From a planning perspective, it will be advantageous for individuals to pay out automobile leases prior to 1994 in order to avoid paying GST on the purchase price, should they wish to purchase the leased car.

Health-care practitioners will also be best off buying their lease equipment prior to 1994 in order to avoid non-recoverable inputs with respect to the subsequent lease payments or a subsequent buy-out.

Note that these rules will not apply when the agreement is varied after the August 8, 1989, effective date.

9. Pre-Paid Rents and Royalties

With the exceptions noted above, pre-paid rents and royalties in 1990 for 1991 supplies will be subject to apportionment rules. They will apply when the pre-payments are made between September 1, 1990, and January 1, 1991, and the vendor of the property is a registrant.

In these circumstances, the amount that is pre-paid will be considered to have been paid after 1990 and will therefore be subject to GST in the ordinary course.

10. Transportation

Special transitional rules will apply to transportation of individuals and freight during periods that straddle the implementation date.

When passenger travel begins before 1991 and is completed before February 1991, the cost will not be subject to GST, as long as it is invoiced before May 1991. This will be important for the 1990 Christmas travel season.

For travel beginning in 1990 and ending after January 31, 1991, 50% of the cost will be subject to GST. This rule will apply only when invoices are issued or the consideration is actually paid between September 1, 1990, and January 1, 1991.

In all other circumstances, travel straddling implementation will be subject to full GST rates.

Transportation passes (i.e., bus passes) are subject to the ordinary pro-rating rules when they apply to periods beginning before 1991 and extending after January 1991. For the rule to apply, the payment for the pass must be made or invoiced before May 1991. If not, the full amount of the pass will be subject to GST.

Freight transportation that begins prior to 1991 and extends into 1991 will not be subject to GST if invoiced or paid prior to May 1991.

If the freight transportation services are totally provided in 1991, they will be subject to GST where they were pre-paid at any time after August 1990 and before 1991.

11. Funeral Services

Funeral services that are provided in 1991 will not be subject to GST if they were provided under a contract executed before September 1, 1990. These services are defined to include providing a plot, coffins and headstones or other property that relates to the burial or cremation of an individual under a funeral service arrangement.

VI. GST Planning: The Practicalities

GST is fundamentally a simple tax. In theory, everything bought is subject to tax. Commercial operations recover the tax, treating it as a cash-flow item and consumers pay the tax, treating it as a cost.

It is the exceptions to the basic principles that can make things complicated.

One thing is clear. Businesses and other entities subject to GST (other than individuals) cannot ignore the opportunities and pitfalls of the system. If they do, the tax can result in lost profits or become a nightmare that partially or wholly limits the ability to compete in the marketplace.

There are a number of key considerations that most registrants will have to deal with on a day-to-day basis, including cash flows and pricing. The character of a vendor and purchaser, either as taxable, zero-rated or exempt will give important insights into motivations under the tax.

Some won't care that tax is payable while others refuse to accept GST as an additional charge to existing pricing. Some will prefer to employ rather than buy outside services.

All in all, the country will have to adjust to a new way of

doing business and to new objectives and goals. The adjustment won't happen overnight, and new business practices will probably take years, if not longer, to become familiar.

A change in business practices like this has not occurred since the beginning of the century when taxation was first introduced. Learning to do business under the new system will take patience and persistence.

1. Pricing

Pricing is the most controversial aspect of the GST and with good cause. Everyone is worried that GST is going to cause massive inflation, leading to a recession.

Although the government can prove statistically that the inflationary effect of the GST is within acceptable limits (a one-time 1.25% increase in the inflation rate), the estimates are based on two very critical beliefs — that the repeal of federal sales tax will result in savings and that those savings will be fully passed on to consumers.

It is not very clear that either of these will happen.

The current sales tax system is badly flawed. It applies unequally and represents a counterproductive cost of manufacturing in Canada. Replacing a flawed tax with a new multi-staged system should theoretically result in savings. Happily, in the majority of cases, the savings should be real, with only a few exceptions.

Potential for price drops and federal sales tax savings will vary, depending on the industry and its related business practices. As a rule of thumb, manufacturers and importers will experience the greatest savings.

Their selling prices were subject to 13.5% tax under the federal sales tax system and will be subject to only 7% under GST. That represents a 6.5% drop in their prices.

Or does it?

Marketing and distribution costs play a role in this analysis. For decades, manufacturers have used marketing and distribution companies to reduce the cost of federal sales tax. The tax scheme was simple. Manufacturers would set up wholly owned marketing and distribution companies. All manufactured goods would be sold to these companies at a fixed profit and federal sales tax would be based on that price. Subsequent sales by the marketing and distribution companies, which incurred the additional selling costs, would not be subject to the tax. Cost would be reduced accordingly, leaving room for competitive pricing and higher profit margins.

Though the federal government tried on several occasions to limit the use of these planning strategies, they continued to proliferate.

Under GST, manufacturers that did not use marketing and distribution companies, or other techniques, to reduce federal sales tax will experience the greatest potential for price savings. They should be in a position to drop prices by the full 6.5% difference between the GST and federal sales taxes.

The same can be said for importers, which sold goods based on duty-paid values that were subject to the tax at the border. In many cases, however, importers mark up prices after importation, or experience additional marketing and distribution costs that drive up the price and reduce the proportion of federal sales tax in relation to that price, reducing the potential for savings under GST.

Manufacturers that used planning to reduce the impact of federal sales tax on their prices will see their potential to reduce prices correspondingly affected.

It will be impossible for purchasers, be they consumers or retailers, to keep track of this potential in light of these factors.

Wholesalers, distributors and retailers will have correspondingly fewer opportunities to drop prices under GST because the federal sales tax component of their prices is proportionately smaller than it is for manufacturers. Further, in order to drop prices to consumers, manufacturers will have to pass federal sales tax savings through to the other trade levels.

If those savings are not passed on, many vendors will not be able to reduce prices to consumers — even if they want to.

Businesses across Canada have been carefully analyzing the impact of potential federal sales tax recoveries. In some cases, operations with sales in the billions are estimated to be facing increased profits in excess of one hundred million if they maintain present price levels.

Although competitive market factors will force some price reductions, it is unlikely that all savings will be passed through to consumers. Instead, it is expected that battles will be waged over who ultimately enjoys these bonanzas, manufacturers, distributors or retailers.

This is one of the potentially fatal flaws in the government's projections on the inflationary impact of GST. Another flaw relates to the timing of savings.

The federal sales tax system has been a mess. Like any good mess, it's going to take a long time to clean up. The effects of federal sales taxes will continue in the system for years after GST is implemented. That is because they cannot be efficiently flushed out of the system immediately on repeal without certain drastic measures that the government is not prepared to take (such as refunding the federal sales tax content of machinery and equipment owned as at January 1, 1991).

The longer the Senate delays passage of the proposed Goods and Services Tax Bill, the greater the chances of double taxation and higher prices for consumers early in 1991.

The Consumer and Corporate Affairs watchdog committee overseeing price gouging by vendors will also have to be careful that it doesn't jump the gun by targeting businesses that are not able to pass on tax savings until months after the GST becomes law.

A majority of businesses are in the middle of pricing products for the 1991 selling year and they don't have enough information about GST to determine whether repeal of the existing manufacturer's sales tax system will result in savings to consumers. If the GST Bill is not passed by the fall of 1990, vendors probably won't be able to pass on savings until months after the January 1, 1991, implementation date.

Pricing does not magically happen overnight. It takes months, even years, of careful planning for pricing issues to be resolved by different businesses. Thousands of vendors across Canada were setting prices for the first and second quarters of 1991 as early as the first and second quarters of 1990. Some have already set prices for the entire 1991 selling year. The fact that GST was not law early in 1990 is causing them real headaches.

Companies that sell by catalogue are probably in the worst spot. They have to fix prices and publish them long before they know whether GST is to become law and what price savings are available as a result of the inventory rebate (the percentage rebate for existing inventories likely won't be known until after the bill becomes law).

It makes for an impossible situation.

If a business publishes prices based on the GST becoming law in 1991 and implementation is delayed (which will probably happen if the bill is not passed by the end of September), it could lose what little profit margins it had when prices under GST will be lower than they are now.

Finance Minister Michael Wilson has not been exaggerating claims that real savings will be available under GST. His claims are premised on the fact that, in some cases, the 13.5% sales tax applied at a manufacturer's level results in higher prices to consumers than a 7% GST charged at a consumer's level.

For example, an automobile manufacturer sells cars to dealers at $10,000, resulting in tax under the present system of $1,350. The dealer adds a $2,000 mark-up and sells the car to a consumer for a total of $13,350.

Under GST, the dealer would buy the car for $10,000 plus $700 of GST. However, because the dealer gets the $700 back as an input tax credit, it would be able to sell the car to a consumer for the net cost of $10,000 plus a $2,000 mark-up. The $12,000 price would be subject to 7% GST ($840) for a total purchase price of $12,840. GST results in savings of $510.

Car dealers will have to be careful quoting prices for 1991 until after the Senate either passes or rejects the Bill. Mistakes will be costly. If the car in the example was advertised for the lower GST-based price and the system did not become law as planned, profits under the federal sales tax system would be reduced by the $510 of anticipated GST savings, about a 25% reduction.

Another pricing problem relates to the proposed inventory rebate. The GST will apply to all sales after implementation, regardless of whether the goods sold had already been subject to the manufacturer's tax.

The proposed inventory rebate is supposed to limit double taxation by refunding the sales tax content of inventories held on January 1, 1991. But it won't. By using seven different rebate percentages instead of rebating the actual tax content of inventories (discussed in Chapter III), the existing sales tax will not be flushed out of the system and GST will apply on top of the manufacturer's tax. It could take the first couple of quarters in 1991 before true price savings are available on a broad range of goods.

Strategies for pricing will be varied, depending on who is doing the buying and who is doing the selling. Consumers will pressure retailers to reduce prices. Retailers will be pressuring wholesalers, distributors and manufacturers to pass on federal sales tax savings. Manufacturers will have to try to find savings and decide if they are to be passed on.

Although competition may force everyone in the supply chain to be honest (as noted above), closely controlled markets may be able to keep federal sales tax savings for themselves.

The impact of compliance costs is also a great unknown. It is unlikely that full federal sales tax savings can be passed on until vendors know how much complying with GST costs. This could take years in some cases. If savings are passed on without taking these costs into account, profit margins will be reduced.

Finally, the impact of profit margin ratios under federal sales tax, in comparison to the GST, have to be analysed.

Prices at trade levels other than manufacturers' trade levels have usually reflected the fact that profit margins are determined on the federal sales tax portion of the cost of goods. Removing federal sales tax means reducing the base on which profit margins are determined. If margins are not determined with GST included in the base, overall profits for some goods may be reduced.

Price reductions under GST will therefore, to a degree, be dependent on the manner in which profit margins are determined and the extent to which margins are reduced to accommodate the removal of federal sales tax factors in cost of goods.

In practical terms, vendors and purchasers will have to understand that a new game is afoot and that they must adjust strategies and practices to accommodate the new market factors. The uninitiated will be the biggest losers.

Careful analysis of market players, their position under federal sales tax and the impact of GST on their practices will be the best protection against exploitation. Take for granted that several years will pass before all the pricing facts and figures are known and the rules of the game have jelled.

From an inflationary perspective, it is unlikely that the government's assumptions (tax savings that are completely passed on to consumers) will be met in their entirety. More serious inflation than was projected could follow.

2. Cash Flows

Cash flow is what GST is all about for taxable commercial and other enterprises. It is the big issue.

Federal sales tax was a "cost" of doing business. It was paid on the selling price of manufactured goods and was not recoverable, except in limited circumstances (i.e., special purpose users, like universities, could obtain refunds). GST is not a cost of doing business. It is recoverable. It is a cash flow item.

In simple terms, businesses will pay GST on all purchases, while collecting tax on all sales. When tax on sales in a reporting period exceeds tax on purchases, the difference will have to be remitted to the government. Alternatively, when GST paid exceed taxes collected (which will normally be the case for zero-rated suppliers, such as food manufacturers) a direct refund of the shortfall will be available.

On the one hand, taxable businesses that owe the government GST will experience an excess of cash equal to the amount to be remitted. On the other hand, businesses expecting refunds are going to have to finance the cost of GST on their purchases until they are recovered.

Like any cash flow item (i.e., a receivable), GST has to be properly managed.

Taxable registrants who collect GST promptly will be able to use the excess cash flow to earn additional profits for a period of time. It depends on how long they can hang on to the money. That means carefully analyzing reporting periods and making choices based on lengthening GST holding periods.

Registrants who are in a position to obtain refunds (such as zero-rated food sellers or real estate developers) have to recover GST inputs as soon as possible. This reduces the cost of financing the GST component of taxes paid on purchases necessary to do business.

There is a lot of money to be made or saved following these simple guidelines and their importance cannot be overemphasized.

For example, assume $100,000 of GST is collected on March 1 by a monthly filer that is obligated to remit the tax on the last day of April, along with its return for that month. If the vendor could earn a 12% return on the funds for 60 days, the cash flow benefits associated with the GST collection would, on a non-compounded basis, equal $1, 972.60.

The larger the operation, the greater the potential earnings in relation to the GST collection and remittance process.

The rule of thumb: The closer to the beginning of a filing period GST is collected, the greater the potential for earnings on that amount.

On the other hand, assume that $100,000 of GST is paid on March 1 by a food vendor that files monthly and must claim a refund on the entire amount. The refund could not be claimed until the return for March was filed, at the end of April. Further, Revenue Canada would not have to start paying interest on the refund until 21 days after the return was received. Assuming an April 30 receipt, interest would begin on May 22, resulting in an 81-day financing period.

If the food vendor was paying 14.5% to finance the GST input, the cost of that exercise would, on a non-compounded basis, be $3,257.53.

The larger the operation, the greater the potential costs of financing GST refunds or rebates.

The rule of thumb in these circumstances: Delaying input credits until the end of a reporting period will reduce carrying costs associated with recovery by way of refund or rebate.

There is a whole range of situations in between those illustrated by these examples. For fully taxable operations, the GST will provide an additional 7% incentive to seek prompt payment of accounts.

Financing costs associated with receivables will be increased by additional GST components.

Operations that are in consistent refund positions, such as food vendors, will be motivated to stage inputs until the end of accounting periods and claim refunds as soon as possible. Taxable operations that do not have regular sales from which GST inputs might be recovered, such as real estate projects that do not experience regular cash flows during the construction phase, will also have similar motivations to reduce exposure to inputs and limit time periods to recovery.

Prudent registrants will constantly monitor cash flow issues in relation to GST to maximize advantages and minimize potential costs.

3. Buying Equipment: Transition Planning

The transition from the federal sales tax system to the GST could artificially distort various industrial markets during 1990 because of opportunities for businesses to save as much as 13.5% in tax.

Unlike consumers, who will have an incentive to purchase expensive items to beat 1991 price increases, many businesses could delay large capital expenditures until after the tax deadline. The opportunities to save tax on capital purchases will exist because of the need to purify existing inventories of their federal sales tax component before imposing the 7% GST. Under the current system, federal sales tax is payable on a manufacturer's sales price of goods.

On January 1, 1991, many businesses will have inventories that include as much as a 13.5% component of federal sales tax (though it is estimated that most will be lower). As noted previously, to allow GST to be imposed on unpurified inventories would result in double taxation. Accordingly, the federal government intends to establish rules to refund manufacturers' tax inherent in those inventories, resulting in the potential to lower selling prices on those inventories (see Chapter V, "Transition," for details of the federal sales tax inventory rebate).

Rebates will not, however, be available for federal sales tax inherent in capital equipment. The absence of refunds for capital equipment could cause businesses to either defer purchases or temporarily rent these items until after the implementation date.

By delaying purchases, it will theoretically be possible to recover GST paid on capital assets as an input credit, while at the same time buying at a price that has been reduced by the federal sales tax refund obtained by a seller.

For example, assume that an advertising firm intends to

computerize its office through the acquisition of hardware with a tax-included capital cost, under the present system, of $1,135,000 purchased directly from a manufacturer and on which $135,000 represents the sales tax component).

If the firm waited until after the implementation of the GST, the initial capital cost of the equipment could theoretically drop to $1,000,000, reflecting the fact that the seller obtained a $135,000 refund of the tax-paid content of its inventory. Though an additional $90,000 in GST would be payable after 1990, the advertising firm could recover the full amount as an input tax credit. In this example, the proposed transitional rules would give the firm a $135,000 incentive to delay computerization until January 1991.

One major problem with the proposed rebates is that it will often be difficult to ascertain with any degree of certainty the exact federal sales tax component that relates to a particular portion of the inventory. Potential savings will be directly tied to the proportionate impact that the generic rebates will have on the vendor's inventory.

In practical terms, large purchases will carry the potential for greater savings under GST. Analysis of a particular situation will provide the information necessary to determine if sales should be delayed until after 1990 for taxable registrants. Short-term solutions, such as rentals, can deal with the problems of equipment shortages until 1991.

Exempt purchasers, on the other hand, will probably want to accelerate equipment purchases to beat implementation. Although the property might be subject to a 13.5% charge on the manufacturer's price, that might be quite a bit less than a 7% charge on a retailer's ultimate selling price.

4. Tax-Exempt Industries

Many industry groups clamoured for exemptions under the GST without really realizing the implications of that request. Some were unlucky enough to get their wish.

The bottom line is that businesses want to be fully taxable under the GST system. That is the only way they can avoid having the tax become an operating cost.

Operations not fully integrated into the system are treated as "consumers," rather than simple tax collectors for the federal government.

To repeat, every commercial transaction, up to and including sales to consumers, will be subject to GST. At each stage, business operations recover taxes paid by way of input tax credits. In this way, they can be viewed as tax collectors, rather than taxpayers. Consumers are the only parties in the tax chain who cannot normally recover the GST component of their purchases.

The term "exemption" under the GST is a bit of a misnomer. It is generally used to refer to the sale of goods and services to consumers free of taxation. However, businesses that sell exempt items will, contrary to the general rule, become fully taxable.

The proposed system will have two types of exceptions. The first one, referred to as "zero-rating," allows businesses to sell goods and services free of GST. At the same time, these vendors are allowed to recover their input taxes.

The second exception, actually called an "exemption," also allows tax-free sales. However, vendors are not entitled to claim input credits. In these circumstances, input taxes are a cost of production that is not directly recoverable.

Thus, for example, should an operation incur $500 of GST to produce $10,000 of goods subject to exemption, it cannot be directly recovered because tax is not collected on the sale. Further, vendors selling exempt goods and services will not be entitled to apply to the government for a refund of their input taxes.

The fact that vendors selling exempted goods and services are not entitled to credits under the proposed system will not stop them from indirectly recovering the GST they have paid out by increasing prices. Thus, even though consumers will theoretically be buying these items free from GST, their purchases will not be entirely tax free.

Rather, only the retail level of sale (and margins associated with that level) will be exempted from the tax. Depending on the industry involved, as much as 90% or more of the cost of an exempted item could be subject to GST.

A number of services are subject to exemption status. These include health care and dental services, education and daycare. Residential rents and used housing will also escape taxation in this way.

All vendors engaged in these services will have difficulties with being exempted, not only because they become consumers of the tax, but also because of the compliance headaches associated with segregating exempt and taxable sales. In some cases, the compliance problems can be severe. Universities, for example, will be hard hit. They will have taxable, zero-rated and exempt activities. They will have to keep track of and reasonably allocate inputs among these activities. For large universities, with $100-million budgets, this process can become impossible. If done improperly (such as when inputs that can be recovered on allocation to taxable activities are not kept track of), losses can be large.

Certain regulated industries will be badly caught by their exemption status. The medical profession will be the hardest hit group. Other groups that rely on government-funded fixed-fee schedules, such as medical laboratory testing operations, could also be caught in this vise.

The real problem with the exemption method for regulated industries is that they may not be in a position to increase the price of their goods or services to recover the tax. Instead, the GST component of their purchases will represent a true non-recoverable cost, reducing profits accordingly. Once again, the the medical profession provides us with a good example. Under the present medicare system, doctors bill provincial health services plans for their services. Their fees are based on regulated schedules that have been very inflexible to increases. It is improbable that these provincial bodies will be prepared to accommodate the additional cost of GST incurred by doctors. As a consequence, doctors can expect that their net profits will be reduced by 7% of the cost of their taxable purchases (basically everything but labour).

Financial institutions will also be exempted in relation to some of their services. However, they will be able to increase prices to consumers in order to recover input taxes indirectly.

In some cases, the financial institutions will try to limit input credits on their exempt activities by hiring employees to perform functions that were previously purchased from outside consultants. Rather than using external law firms, banks may increase internal legal departments and save the input taxes associated with external legal fees.

Exempt industries will have to carefully monitor the impact of non-recoverable inputs, as well as the costs of compliance associated with distinguishing and allocating between taxable and exempt sales. Indirect means of recovery will have to be found to limit erosion of existing profit margins.

Refer to the Appendix for a legislative description of exempt activities.

5. Zero-Rated Industries

Zero-rated industries are comparable to fully taxable industries (i.e., tax is charged on the sale and input credits are recoverable), except in one respect. GST is charged at a rate of zero.

Zero-rated industries exist for technical reasons. It is a method of excepting certain supplies from any direct or indirect GST charges. Although exempt supplies are not subject to tax on sale, inputs cannot be claimed as credits in the system. This often forces increased prices to purchasers as an indirect method of recovering the tax. This doesn't happen with zero-rating. With few exceptions, zero-rated products should be totally GST free.

A number of supplies have been zero-rated for social policy reasons. These include prescription drugs, basic groceries, exports, travel and transportation services. Refer to the Appendix for a complete legislative listing of the zero-rated goods and services.

Consumers will therefore have an incentive to buy zero-rated supplies over either taxable or exempted supply.

Taxable purchasers other than consumers will also be happy to buy zero-rated supplies. Unlike taxable supplies, they won't have to wait to get the GST back as an input credit.

Who will want to be zero-rated? Most likely exempt registrants that want to be excepted from the system but also want to recover input credits.

Zero-rated suppliers will have an incentive, for cash-flow purposes, to recover input taxes as quickly as possible. While the taxes remain outstanding, they increase financing costs (see "Cash Flows," earlier in this chapter, for more details).

Zero-rated industries also have an incentive, for cash-flow purposes, to employ people to perform tasks that would otherwise be purchased from outside sources. In this way, the extra cost of financing GST inputs for purchased services can be reduced or eliminated.

From a compliance perspective, zero-rated registrants will have to distinguish among taxable, exempt and zero-rated sales. Purchasers will also have to identify zero-rated supplies in order that input credits not be claimed on those goods or services.

The taxation of food is perhaps the most controversial aspect of the GST.

On the one hand, there are the political concerns. Political theory suggests that taxing food can severely limit the ability of the incumbent government to be re-elected. It is hard to imagine that this consideration was not seriously addressed in the decision to except food from tax.

On the other hand, there are theoretical concerns. A multistage consumption tax is most efficient when it applies uniformly, without exception. A major exclusion, like food, will distort the system, driving up tax rates.

Finally, there are the practical concerns. The cost of excluding food is overwhelming. It is theorized that food prices will artificially increase to accommodate the cost of exclusion under the GST, defeating the point of the exception.

The practical aspects of taxing food under the GST are the most pressing public concern. They include:

- The creation of a massive bureaucracy, both by government and the private sector, to develop and monitor the methodology of distinguishing between tax-free and taxable food.
- The replacement of capital equipment, such as cash registers, computers and handling systems that must be designed to accommodate the imposition of GST, as well as the segregation of taxable and tax-free food.
- The development of new accounting procedures and inventory controls, with the attendant need to revise computer software systems, to conform with GST requirements and differentiate between inconsistent federal and provincial sales taxes.
- The creation of biases against certain types of food, such as prepared meals, which attract taxation, in favour of non-taxable supply.

It has been estimated that these costs alone (ignoring the losses of small businesses that cannot cope with the compliance costs and reporting requirements) will be measured in hundreds of millions of dollars, which will be available to be added to the cost of both taxable and non-taxable food items.

It was therefore not hard to sympathize with Finance Minister Wilson's inclination to seriously consider the taxation of food, particularly when other, less controversial and costly, methods of accomplishing the primary objectives of excepting food are available.

Simultaneously, social policy and political reality could be satisfied by using existing systems to reimburse certain sectors of society for the imposition of tax on food.

For example, the income tax system could be modified to repatriate the cost of tax on food. This might be accomplished by providing tax credits and refunds on an annual basis through income tax returns, as many provinces presently do in relation to the cost of rental housing.

At the same time, employee source deductions could be reduced to provide direct tax relief on a more immediate basis. Family allowance and the welfare system could also be commandeered to funnel GST relief.

From a social policy perspective, the use of these alternatives would allow the government to direct relief to those segments of society that needed it most, one of the main goals of excepting food from tax.

These methods have not been chosen on implementation of the system, but could present alternatives in the future should the exception of food from the system by way of zero-rating become impossibly unwieldy and unworkable.

Under zero-rating, food vendors will face a significant practical problem — delineating between taxable and zero-rated food. Thousands of new food products are produced each year. Someone is going to have to determine which are taxable and which are not.

When mistakes are made, the food vendors will have to pay the GST that should have been collected by customers. The costs could be enormous if large-volume sales are involved (such as those made by a national supermarket chain that sells taxable items as zero-rated for months or years before an audit).

The costs associated with mistakes, coupled with particularly slim profit margins in the food industry, will provide food vendors with an incentive to keep in close contact with Revenue Canada for guidance on new products before sale.

6. Selling to Governments

The federal government is the largest purchaser of goods and services in Canada. Its purchases represent billions of dollars of commerce annually.

The federal government has an incentive to self-supply under GST and that bias could irrevocably damage the government supply industry. Some market players could disappear overnight if the bias is not counteracted.

Taxing government purchases is regressive and illogical in one sense. It is similar to moving change from one pocket to another. In practical terms, however, it facilitates the mechanical operation of a multi-stage tax like the GST, cutting down on exceptions to the system. Every exception to the system represents a cost in terms of compliance.

The government has therefore chosen to be fully taxable on its purchases to allow the public to avoid the headaches associated with treating government sales as an extraordinary item. There are enough compliance problems in the system without that one.

Each government department will be reimbursed for the cost of GST through an internal system of rebates, referred to by some as "equalization payments." Theoretically, these payments will make the GST component of government purchases a non-event. The government supply industry is worried that will not be the case in practice.

The way in which equalization payments are made can be a problem. If they are done on a percentage basis, rather than rebates of actual GST inputs, the opportunity for bias is stronger.

The government's system of accounting will also work towards creating a self-supply bias. Under that system, recovery of GST inputs will not be linked to actual tax liabilities. An incentive will therefore be created to reduce GST inputs in order to limit spending figures that will not give account to recovery of those inputs by way of equalization payments.

Take a simple example of food services (subject to tax, rather than zero-rated like basic food supplies). Prior to GST, the supply of food services was a tendering process that was balanced on very narrow factors. It was not unheard of for private sector supply contracts to be lost over a matter of a few percentage points of cost. Under GST, 7% will be added to that cost. Purchasing agents will have a psychological incentive to reduce their departmental costs by saving GST on outside supplies and using internal sources that are not subject to the tax.

At the same time, it is possible that equalization payments will not be reduced to fully reflect the use of internal supply. Thus, using internal sources of supply could, in some cases, result in saved GST and recovery of notional taxes through equalization payments.

To handle this bias in New Zealand, inter-departmental purchases by government were subject to GST. A similar system has not been implemented in Canada.

Vendors selling to governments must be aware of the interplay of these new factors that will probably find their way into the tendering process. They can be counteracted with competitive pricing that represents more efficient supply than that available through government sources.

Selling to provincial governments will carry similar problems. It is anticipated that the full-taxation method of excepting the provinces from the GST (i.e., full tax on purchases and recovery by way of federal government transfer payments) will carry the same bias to avoid GST through internal self-supply.

The self-supply bias with provinces may, however, be greater than with the federal government because transfer payments may not result in 100% recovery of inputs to the provinces. If this occurs, provincial purchasing agents will have a greater incentive to reduce input tax burdens.

Note that buying from governments will be the same as buying from taxable vendors. This is necessary to ensure that government sources of supply are not given a competitive advantage over the private sector marketplace sources.

7. The Provinces: Retail Sales Tax and GST

Will the provinces join the federal government in a unified GST scheme? They'd be crazy not to, from an economic perspective. In addition, it won't be long before the public is putting enormous pressure on the provinces to sign up.

Political dogma aside, having a provincial retail sales tax system that operates independently from a national GST is going to be a real nightmare. Compliance will be a constant thorn in the side of taxable registrants.

As far as public revenue, the provinces are losing significant revenues by not expanding the present, relatively limited, retail sales tax base to the broadly based multi-stage tax on goods and services. Rates can drop significantly when the tax base is increased.

Another problem is administration. Hundreds of millions of dollars will be spent administering both types of tax systems. Those costs can be almost entirely saved with an integrated federal-provincial GST, leaving significant additional revenues for things like deficit reduction and social programs.

In the final analysis, it does not make sense to have two disparate systems, either politically, socially or economically. It is unlikely they will remain unintegrated in the long term.

8. Banks, Insurance Companies and Financial Services

Financial services are listed as exempt supplies (see the Appendix for a detailed listing) and are therefore not taxable on their sale. However, input taxes cannot be recovered on those sales. Accordingly, it can be expected that the cost of financial services will increase in order to indirectly recover the cost of input tax associated with the supply of those services.

Accepting deposits, lending funds and all associated services (such as chequing services, administering accounts and credit cards) will be exempt from GST. Other services, such as investment advice, providing cheques, data processing and safety deposit boxes, will generally be taxable.

Most types of insurance policies are also exempted from GST. The main policies exempted include life insurance, as well as property and casualty insurance issued by licensed insurers. For this purpose, reinsurance policies, annuity contracts and segregated fund contracts are defined as insurance policies. Accident and sickness insurance policies are exempted whether or not they are issued by licensed insurers.

Other types of insurance — product warranty, for example — are subject to tax, except to the extent they are made available by a licensed insurer.

The reason for exempting financial services is technical. Few countries employing multi-stage sales taxes have been able to resolve the practical difficulties associated with determining what portion of a financial service supply should be subject to tax.

It is often difficult, given the diversity of this supply, to identify and segregate or even isolate transactions that give rise to tax. In light of these difficulties, financial services have been exempted. Should a pragmatic solution one day become possible, financial services will probably be subjected to tax.

9. Revenue Canada's Helping Hand

Revenue Canada has no intention of letting the proposed Goods and Services Tax become an administrative nightmare. It has taken the bull by the horns by establishing a special group determined to make sure implementation is a textbook exercise.

The GST has the potential to hit business and other private sector members (such as charities, clubs, hospitals and schools) like a steam roller. Although public attention has focused almost entirely on big-picture issues, such as rates and the taxation of food, the reality is that its administration will carry the most significant practical impact for years to come.

One thing is clear. There is not enough time in 1990 for the entire country to become ready for the new system.

Here are some of the biggest problems to watch out for:

- Registration. Taxpayers will have to be signed up under the new system. Until they are, they will not be entitled to a number of incentives that benefit business. These include refunds of federal sales tax on inventories held at the end of 1990; cash grants allowing small business to upgrade cash registers; and the most important, refunds of input tax credits in the system's early stages.

- Collection and remittance. A large number of taxpayers under the GST have never had to collect or remit any kind of tax on their sales. Though retailers are familiar with provincial sales tax and manufacturers have paid federal sales tax for decades, few service industries have encountered direct taxation on their sales. In Alberta, even retailers have no experience with sales tax, leaving some to suggest that this province will have the hardest time accommodating new accounting and inventory controls. Small businessmen, in particular, will have to make serious adjustments in their operations. Although some might avoid compliance by claiming the small business exemption (where annual sales are less than $30,000), most will want to be in the system to recover GST paid on their purchases.
- Integration with provincial sales tax. Nine provinces currently charge a sales tax at different rates and on different products. It will be a constant battle keeping tax liabilities segregated between retail sales tax on some items and GST on others.
- Inventory control. National operations, such as Eaton's and Canadian Tire, will probably have to develop inventory controls that rival space-shuttle software for complexity. Food will cause the most problems. It will be almost impossible to consistently segregate between taxable and zero-rated food, taking into account provincial sales tax variances. Mistakes will be costly when they are not discovered for years, giving rise to the potential for large reassessments.
- Transition. On January 1, 1991, the GST will apply to every contract and legal arrangement in existence, regardless of the

time they were signed (such as a 99-year lease that was signed at the turn of the century). The problem is that many, if not most, of those agreements do not address taxes. As a result, it will be unclear which party has to bear the tax burden. Everything will be fine if GST is charged on the gross selling price. Although purchasers pay the tax, they will recover it as an input tax credit. In this way, a vendor will still receive the same returns that were experienced before the GST was introduced. On the other hand, if GST is payable as part of the gross contract price, vendors will find that they receive less because purchasers recover the tax. The courts could be busy for years resolving these disputes.

A GST "Fix It" committee (officially named the GST Consultation Group) has been crisscrossing the country, digging out problems and helping the private sector find solutions. In Revenue Canada's view, the consultation group will be vital to a successful GST.

Its mandate is to consult with key industry groups, as well as individual businesses, in an effort to identify compliance problems and other administrative issues. Once identified, the group will take the public's suggestions and work with other sections of Revenue Canada to find and implement realistic solutions.

The Fix It committee is already into a second phase. In its first phase, it contacted about 35 key industry groups asking for briefs on problems their members might experience. In its second phase, the group will contact a second tranche of more than 200 industry groups to get their input on GST problems.

Revenue Canada has studied visitation programs in other countries that implemented a consumption tax like the GST and concluded that it is vital to a successful introduction. Studies have shown that one of the main reasons New Zealand had to delay its consumption tax by six months was because of the lack of a visitation program.

The Fix It committee has enjoyed significant success in the

design of the GST registration package. Even though signing up is voluntary until legislation is passed, the government is encouraging the step so that incentives can be available early.

The consultation group has worked with the private sector and Revenue Canada to produce a one-page registration form, almost unheard of in this age of increasing tax complexity.

The group is also unique for the alliances it has been forging with the private sector, not the usual approach Revenue Canada is known for.

In practical terms, it's important to know the channels in government through which problems can be resolved. It is clear there will be a lot of them from an administrative perspective, and only the government will be able to grant administrative concessions or change the law to resolve them.

10. GST and Free Trade

A real problem with the federal sales tax system from an international trade perspective has been the favourable treatment afforded to imported goods in comparison to the application of the tax to domestically manufactured goods. This has often provided imported goods, including those from the United States, with a price advantage in the Canadian marketplace that domestically manufactured goods could not match.

In some price-sensitive market sectors, the competitive advantage available to imported goods has acted as a barrier to domestic manufacturers that could not match pricing. These advantages have been in place for decades and structural flaws inherent in the system have prevented the implementation of interim measures designed to solve the problem.

Under the GST, imports will not be treated any more favourably than domestically manufactured goods.

Thus, while free trade between Canada and the United States will operate to remove barriers to commercial activity between the two countries, the replacement of the federal sales tax with a

GST will likely result in the removal of tax concessions that products manufactured in the United States have enjoyed most of this century.

On the positive side, the GST will apply equally to all industrial sectors in Canada, removing commodity taxes as a competitive cost factor. The playing field will be levelled once again.

U. S. enterprises that produce goods through subsidiaries or branches in Canada will find opportunities for increased margins and market share. Previously unattainable markets may also become available where goods are particularly susceptible to pricing.

Thus, in this respect, the GST will enhance the objectives of free trade, by removing barriers to domestic production in Canada by United States entities.

Almost since its introduction in 1924, the federal sales tax system has been a bane to manufacturers. No fewer than three royal commissions-the Rowell-Sirois Commission in 1940, the Carter Commission in 1966 and most recently the Goodman Committee in 1983- have addressed its fundamental flaws. Each study recommended that the system be materially changed.

A manufacturer or producer is primarily liable to collect and remit the tax on the selling price of goods they fabricate. Several key points are consistently identified as flaws intrinsic to the system. It is argued that:

- The tax is too narrowly based. Since it applies only to some goods, a bias is created to discourage the production of taxable goods in favour of non-taxable items. The narrow base also results in higher rates of taxation, which distort natural economic progression.
- The tax does not uniformly apply to products in different market sectors, or to competing products in the same markets. Some manufacturers can reduce their sale price for tax purposes by excluding marketing and distribution costs in any number of ways. Since not all competitors in an industry

sector can follow suit, disproportionate federal sales tax liabilities warp competition.

- Federal sales tax increases the cost of exports. Although export sales are notionally exempt from taxation, goods and materials used to create those products are inherently subject to tax. Estimates place this inherent cost at more than 10% of an exporter's profit margin, providing incentives for manufacturers to pursue offshore sources of supply not subject to this hidden cost.
- Imports are preferentially treated by the system because no hidden tax is included in the cost of those products. Subsequent marketing and distribution costs are excluded from the tax calculation, unlike most competing goods that are domestically manufactured.

A 1985 study commissioned by the Department of Finance focused on these issues in relation to a broad category of goods. Looking at imports, it was determined that the effective rate of sales tax on domestic goods was 70% to 80% higher than the rate on rival imports.

On the other hand, a review of domestically manufactured goods revealed inconsistent application of the tax resulting in a wide disparity between the effective rate imposed on the same goods produced by competitors. For example, some sporting goods manufacturers are subject to as much as three and one-half times the rate of federal sales tax paid by their rivals in the same marketplace.

These problems have not been assisted by the more than 22,000 private Revenue Canada rulings that attempted to deal with the inequitable application of the tax over the last 60 years. Instead, they have added to its inconsistent application and complexity.

The GST will do away with all of these problems. Since it is a revenue-neutral tax, it will apply equally to all taxable industries, as well as competitors in the same market. Manufacturers will no longer be able to gain unfair advantages by reorganizing their operations to reduce tax.

Imports will be equally treated and the cost of goods produced for export will not be increased by hidden taxes. The private rulings system should disappear overnight (to the relief of both taxpayers and the public service).

The selling price of manufactured goods will be reduced. Market competition should eventually see this reduction passed to the consumer level.

Wholesalers and retailers will be entitled to a refund of the federal sales tax component in their inventories, a one-time windfall when the GST becomes law. Industry competition will again likely pass these recoveries on to consumers.

Though the GST is expected to result in inflation (principally because of the application of GST to a broad range of presently exempt goods and services), some theorize that the removal of existing competitive barriers could result in more jobs, leading to eventual prosperity.

From a planning perspective, the replacement of federal sales tax with GST will provide manufacturers and importers with the opportunity to increase their margins by keeping prices at current levels. By doing so, their gross selling price to suppliers will be increased by GST and ultimately to customers.

However, manufacturers will benefit by recovering the component of the selling price that previously represented federal sales taxes.

Will GST facilitate the free trade arrangements between Canada and the United States ?

On balance, it probably will. Although imported goods may be subject to increased competition, U. S. enterprises operating in Canada, either as branches or subsidiaries, will find they are treated more equitably under the new regime. Opportunities for market share and cash-flow benefits will be equally available for all competitors in the same markets, regardless of whether they are controlled by Canadian or United States parents.

Better tax systems result in increased productivity and profits. If this theory holds, even in part, the GST will be good for both countries.

Appendix: Legislative Materials

Zero-rated and exempt transactions are subject to special rules in the GST system. The legislation has been organized to exclude tax on exempt supplies, with a corresponding removal of entitlement to input tax credits in respect of purchases that relate to those sales. Similarly, zero-rated sales are subjected to tax, but at a rate of nil. This allows vendors to recover their inputs in respect of those sales.

Zero-rating and exemptions are not defined in the body of the legislation. Rather, schedules are attached as appendices to the law as a means of identifying those activities that fall into these categories. These schedules are reproduced below and should be referred to for specific details on which activities and transactions attract these characterizations. Reference should be made to the various chapters in the book that deal with these topics for more substantive discussion of the use to which the schedules should be put.

Another important aspect of the legislation is the numerous definitions included at the beginning of the GST Bill. The definitions set the stage for the application of the rules and regulations in a variety of circumstances. They are also reproduced as a guide with respect to the application of the rules in particular situations.

The following appendices contain several sections of the GST Bill (C-62), which are useful in determining the status of a particular supply, be it taxable, zero-rated or exempt. They also contain definitions that are critical to the understanding of the system.

On May 14, 1990 the Department of Finance issued explanatory notes on the GST Bill. Excerpts from these notes are also included in the appendices. These notes do not, however, carry the force of law. As a result, they only represent guides to the intended interpretation and application of a particular provision to which they relate.

DIVISION I

INTERPRETATION

Definitions

123. (1) In section 121, this Part and Schedules V, VI and VII.

"admission"

"admission," in respect of a place of amusement or a seminar, an activity or an event, means a right of entry or access to, or attendance at, the place of amusement or the seminar, activity or event;

"amount"

"amount" means money, property or a service, expressed in terms of the amount of money or the value in terms or money of the property or service;

"assessment"

"assessment" means an assessment under this Part and includes a reassessment under this Part;

"builder"

"builder" of a residential complex or of an addition to a multiple unit residential complex means a person who

(*a*) at a time when the person has an interest in the real property on which the complex is situated, carries on or engages another person to carry on for the person

(i) in the case of an addition to a multiple unit residential complex, the construction of the addition to the multiple unit residential complex,

(ii) in the case of a residential condominium unit, the construction of the condominium complex in which the unit is situated, and

(iii) in any other case, the construction or substantial renovation of the complex,

(*b*) acquires an interest in the complex at a time when

(i) in the case of an addition to a multiple unit residential complex, the addition is under construction, and

(ii) in any other case, the complex is under construction or substantial renovation,

(*c*) in the case of a mobile home,

(*d*) acquires an interest in the complex

(i) in the case of a condominium complex or residential condominium unit, at a time when the complex is not registered as a condominium, or

(ii) in any case, before it has been occupied by an individual as a place of residence or lodging under any arrangement for that purpose,

for the primary purpose of making a supply of the complex or any part thereof or an interest therein by way of sale, or

(*e*) a person deemed under subsection 190(1) to be a builder of the complex, but does not include an individual described in any of paragraphs (*a*) to (*d*) who carries on the construction or substantial renovation, or acquires the complex or interest therein, otherwise than in the course of a business or an adventure or concern in the nature of trade or a person described in any of paragraphs (*a*) to (*c*) whose interest in the complex is a right to purchase the complex from a builder of the complex;

"business"

"business" includes a profession, calling, trade, manufacture or undertaking of any kind whatever, whether the activity or undertaking is engaged in for profit, and any activity engaged in on a regular or continuous basis that involves the supply of property by way of lease, licence or similar arrangement, but does not include an office or employment;

"calendar quarter"

"calendar quarter" means a period of three months beginning on the first day of January, April, July or October in each calendar year;

"capital property" "capital property," in respect of a person, means property that is, or would be if the person were a taxpayer under the *Income Tax Act*, capital property of the person within the meaning of the Act, other than property described in Class 12 or 14 of Schedule II to the *Income Tax Regulations*;

"charity" "charity" means a registered charity or registered Canadian amateur athletic association, within the meaning of the *Income Tax Act*;

"closely related group" "closely related group" means a group of corporations each member of which is closely related, within the meaning assigned by section 128, to each other member of the group;

"commercial activity" "commercial activity" means

(*a*) any business carried on by a person,

(*b*) any adventure or concern of a person in the nature of trade, and

(*c*) any activity engaged in by a person that involves the supply of real property or of a right or interest in respect of real property by that person,

but does not include

(*d*) any activity engaged in by a person to the extent that it involves the making of an exempt supply by the person,

(*e*) any activity engaged in by an individual without a reasonable expectation of profit, or

(*f*) the performance of any duty or activity in relation to an office or employment;

"condominium complex" "condominium complex" means a residential complex that contains more than one residential condominium unit;

"consideration fraction" "consideration fraction" means 100/107;

"consumer" "consumer" of property or a service means a particular individual who acquires or imports the property or service for the particular individual's personal consumption, use or enjoyment or the personal consumption, use or enjoyment of any other individual at the particular individual's expense, but does not include an individual who acquires or imports the property or service for consumption, use or supply in the course of commercial activities of the individual or other activities in the course of which the individual makes exempt supplies;

"credit note" "credit note" means a note issued under subsection 232(3);

"credit union" "credit union" has the meaning assigned by subsection 137(6) of the *Income Tax Act* and includes a corporation described in subparagraph 137.1(5)(*a*)(i) of that Act;

"debt security" "debt security" means a right to be paid money and includes a deposit of money, but does not include a lease, licence or similar arrangement for the use of, or the right to use, property other than a financial instrument;

"Department" "Department" means the Department of National Revenue;

"Deputy Minister" "Deputy Minister" means the Deputy Minister of National Revenue for Customs and Excise;

"document" "document" includes money, a security and a record;

"equity security" "equity security" means a share of the capital stock of a corporation or any interest in or right to such a share;

"excisable goods" "excisable goods" means any goods on which a duty of excise is imposed under the *Excise Act* or would be imposed under that Act if the goods were manufactured or produced in Canada;

"exclusive" "exclusive," in respect of the consumption, use or supply of property or a service, means all or substantially all of the consumption, use or supply of the property or service, and "all or substantially all," in respect of the consumption, use or supply of property or a service by a financial institution, means all of the consumption, use or supply of the property or service;

"exempt supply" "exempt supply" means a supply included in Schedule V;

"export" "export" means export from Canada;

"fair market value" "fair market value" of property or a service supplied to a person means the fair market value of the property or service without reference to any tax excluded by section 154 from the consideration for the supply;

"financial institution" "financial institution," at any time, means a person who is at that time a financial institution under section 149;

"financial instrument" "financial instrument" means

(*a*) a debt security,

(*b*) an equity security,

(*c*) an insurance policy,

(*d*) an interest in a partnership or trust or any right in respect of such an interest,

(*e*) a precious metal,

(*f*) an option or a contract for the future supply of a commodity, where the option or contract is traded on a recognized commodity exchange,

(*g*) a prescribed instrument,

(*h*) a guarantee, an acceptance or an indemnity in respect of anything described in paragraph (*a*), (*b*), (*d*), (*e*) or (*g*), or

(i) an option or a contract for the future supply of money or anything described in any of paragraphs (*a*) to (*h*);

"financial service" "financial service" means

(*a*) the exchange, payment, issue, receipt or transfer of money, whether effected by the exchange of currency, by crediting or debiting accounts or otherwise,

(*b*) the operation or maintenance of a savings, chequing, deposit, loan, charge or other account,

(*c*) the lending or borrowing of a financial instrument,

(*d*) the issue, granting, allotment, acceptance, endorsement, renewal, processing, variation, transfer of ownership or repayment of a financial instrument,

(*e*) the provision, variation, release or receipt of a guarantee, an acceptance or an indemnity in respect of a financial instrument,

(*f*) the payment or receipt of dividends (other than dividends in kind and patronage dividends), interest, principal, claims, benefits or any other amount in respect of a financial instrument,

(*g*) the making of any advance, the granting of any credit or the lending of money,

(*h*) the underwriting of a financial instrument,

(*i*) any service provided pursuant to the terms and conditions of any agreement relating to payments of amounts for which a credit card voucher or charge card voucher has been issued,

(*j*) the service of investigating and recommending the compensation in satisfaction of a claim arising under an insurance policy provided by an insurer or by a person licensed under the laws of a province to carry on such services,

(*k*) any supply deemed by sub-

section 150(1) or section 158 to be a supply of a financial service,
(*l*) the agreeing to provide, or the arranging for, a service referred to in any of paragraphs (*a*) to (i), or
(*m*) a prescribed service,

but does not include
(*n*) the payment or receipt of money as consideration for the supply of property other than a financial instrument or of a service other than a financial service,
(O) the payment or receipt of money in settlement of a claim (other than a claim under an insurance policy) under a warranty, guarantee or similar arrangement in respect of property other than a financial instrument or a service other than a financial service,
(*p*) the service of providing advice other than a service included in this definition by reason of paragraph (*j*),
(*q*) the provision of management or administrative services to a corporation, partnership or trust the principal activity of which is the investing of funds on behalf of shareholders, members or other persons,
(*r*) a professional service provided by an accountant, actuary, lawyer or notary in the course of a professional practice,
(*s*) any service the supply of which is deemed under this Part to be a taxable supply, or
(*t*) a prescribed service;

"fiscal month" "fiscal month" of a person means a period that is determined under section 243 to be the fiscal month of the person;

"fiscal quarter" "fiscal quarter" of a person means a period that is determined under section 243 to be the fiscal quarter of the person;

"fiscal year" "fiscal year" of a person means
(*a*) where the person has made an election under section 244 that is in effect, the period that the person elected to be the fiscal year of the person, and
(*b*) in all other cases, the taxation year of the person;

"former spouse" "former spouse" of a particular individual includes an individual of the opposite sex with whom the particular individual cohabited in a conjugal relationship;

"game of chance" "game of chance" means a lottery or other scheme under which prizes or winnings are awarded by way of chance or by way of a mixture of chance and other factors where the result depends more on chance than on the other factors;

"goods" "goods" has the same meaning as in the *Customs Act*;

"government" "government" means Her Majesty in right of Canada or a province;

"hospital authority" "hospital authority" means an organization or that part of an organization that operates a public hospital that is certified as such by the Department of National Health and Welfare;

"import" "import" means import into Canada;

"improvement" "improvement," in respect of capital property of a person, means any property or service that is supplied to, or goods that are imported by, the person for the purpose of improving the capital property, to the extent that the consideration paid or payable by the person for the property or service or the value of the goods is, or would be if the person were a taxpayer under the *Income Tax*

Act, included in determining the adjusted cost base to the person of the capital property for the purposes of that Act;

"individual" — "individual" means a natural person;

"insurance policy" — "insurance policy" means

(*a*) a policy or contract of insurance that is issued by an insurer, including

(i) a policy of reinsurance issued by an insurer,

(ii) an annuity contract issued by an insurer, or a contract issued by an insurer that would be an annuity contract except that the payments under the contract

(*A*) are payable on a periodic basis at intervals that are longer or shorter than one year, or

(*B*) vary in amount depending on the value of a specified group of assets or on changes in interest rates, and

(iii) a contract issued by an insurer all or part of the insurer's reserves for which vary in amount depending on the value of a specified group of assets, and

(*b*) a policy or contract in the nature of accident, sickness or dental insurance, whether the policy is issued, or the contract is entered into, by an insurer;

"insurer" — "insurer" means a person who is licensed or otherwise authorized under the laws of Canada or a province to carry on in Canada an insurance business or under the laws of another jurisdiction an insurance business;

"invoice" — "invoice" includes a statement of account, a bill and any other similar record, regardless of its form or characteristics, and a cash register slip or receipt;

"listed financial institution" — "listed financial institution" means a person referred to in paragraph 149(1)(*a*);

"membership" — "membership" includes a right granted by a particular person that entitles another person to services that are provided by, or to the use of facilities that are operated by, the particular person and that are not available, or are not available to the same extent or for the same fee or charge, to persons to whom such a right has not been granted, and also includes such a right where it is provided under the terms and conditions of a share, bond, debenture or other security issued by a person;

"mineral" — "mineral" includes petroleum, natural gas and related hydrocarbons and sand and gravel;

"Minister" — "Minister" means the Minister of National Revenue;

"mobile home" — "mobile home" means a unit that is not less than three metres wide and eight metres long, that is equipped with complete plumbing, electrical and heating facilities and that is designed to be towed on its own chassis on wheels to a site for installation on a foundation and connection to service facilities at that site and to be occupied for residential purposes, but does not include any freestanding appliances or furniture sold with the unit or any travel trailer, motor home, camping trailer or other vehicle or trailer for recreational use;

"money" — "money" includes any currency, cheque, promissory note, letter of credit, draft, traveller's cheque, bill of exchange, postal note, money order, postal remittance and other similar instrument, whether Canadian or foreign, but does not include currency the fair market value of which exceeds its stated value as legal tender in the country of issuance or currency that is supplied or held for its numismatic value;

"multiple unit residential complex" — "multiple unit residential complex" means a residential complex that contains more than one residential unit, but does not include a condominium complex;

"municipality" — "municipality" means
(*a*) an incorporated city, town, village, metropolitan authority, township, district, county or rural municipality or other incorporated municipal body however designated, and
(*b*) such other local authority as the Minister may determine to be a municipality for the purposes of this Part;

"non-profit organization" — "non-profit organization" means a person (other than an individual, an estate, a trust or a charity) that was organized and is operated solely for a purpose other than profit, no part of the income of which is payable to, or otherwise available for the personal benefit of any proprietor, member or shareholder thereof unless the proprietor, member or shareholder is a club, a society or an association the primary purpose and function of which is the promotion of amateur athletics in Canada;

"non-resident" — "non-resident" means not resident in Canada;

"officer" — "officer" includes
(*a*) a member of the board of directors, board of management or other governing board of a corporation, society, union, club, association, organization or any other body of any kind whatever,
(*b*) a judicial officer or a member of a judicial, quasi-judicial or administrative board, tribunal or body,
(*c*) a Minister of the Crown in right of Canada or a province,
(*d*) a member of the Senate or House of Commons of Canada
(*e*) a member of legislature of a province, and
(*f*) the incumbent of any other office who is elected or appointed to act as a representative of a group of persons;

"passenger vehicle" — "passenger vehicle" has the meaning assigned by subsection 248(1) of the *Income Tax Act*;

"patronage dividend" — "patronage dividend" means an amount that is deductible under section 135 of the *Income Tax Act* in computing, for the purposes of that Act, the income of the person paying the amount;

"permanent establishment" — "permanent establishment," in respect of a particular person, means
(*a*) a fixed place of business of the particular person, including
(i) a place of management, a branch, and office, a factory or a workshop, and
(ii) a mine, an oil or gas well, a quarry, timberland or any other place of extraction of natural resources, through which the particular person makes supplies, or
(*b*) a fixed place of business of another person (other than a broker, general commission agent or other independent agent acting in the ordinary course of business) who is acting in Canada on behalf of the particular person

and through whom the particular person makes supplies in the ordinary course of business;

"person" — "person" means an individual, partnership, corporation, trust or estate, or a body that is a society, union, club, association, commission or other organization of any kind;

"personal property" — "personal property" means property that is not real property;

"place of amusement" — "place of amusement" means any premises or place, whether or not enclosed, at or in any part of which is staged or held any
(*a*) film, slide show, sound and light or similar presentation,
(*b*) artistic, literary, theatrical, musical or other performance, entertainment or exhibition,
(*c*) fair, circus, menagerie, rodeo or similar event, or
(*d*) race, game of chance, athletic contest or other contest or game,
and includes a museum, historical site, zoo, wildlife or other park, place where bets are placed and any place, structure, apparatus, machine or device the purpose of which is to provide any type of amusement or recreation;

"precious metal" — "precious metal" means a bar, ingot, coin or wafer that is composed of gold, silver or platinum and that is refined to a purity level of at least
(*a*) 99.5% in the case of gold and platinum, and
(*b*) 99.9% in the case of silver;

"prescribed" — "prescribed" means
(*a*) in the case of a form, the information to be given on a form or the manner of filing a form, prescribed by the Minister, and
(*b*) in any other case, prescribed by regulation or determined in accordance with rules prescribed by regulation;

"property" — "property" means any property, whether real or personal, movable or immovable, tangible or intangible, corporeal or incorporeal, and includes a right or interest of any kind, a share and a chose in action, but does not include money;

"public college" — "public college" means an organization or that part of an organization that operates a post-secondary college or post-secondary technical institute
(*a*) that is funded by a government or a municipality, and
(*b*) the primary purpose of which is to provide programs of instruction in one or more fields of vocational, technical or general education;

"public sector body" — "public sector body" means a government or a public service body;

"public service body" — "public service body" means a non-profit organization, a charity, a municipality, a school authority, a hospital authority, a public college or a university;

"qualifying subsidiary" — "qualifying subsidiary" of a particular corporation means another corporation resident in Canada not less than 90% of the value and number of the issued and outstanding shares of the capital stock of which, having full voting rights under all circumstances, are owned by the particular corporation, and includes
(*a*) a corporation that is a qualifying subsidiary of a qualifying subsidiary of the particular corporation, and
(*b*) where the particular corporation is a credit union, every other credit union;

"real property" — "real property" includes
(*a*) in respect of property in the Province of Quebec, immovable property and every lease thereof,

(*b*) in respect of property in any other place in Canada, messuages, lands and tenements of every nature and description and every estate or interest in real property, whether legal or equitable, and
(*c*) a mobile home;

"recipient" "recipient," in respect of a supply, means the person who pays or agrees to pay consideration for the supply or, if no consideration is or is to be paid for the supply, the person to whom the supply is made;

"record" "record" includes a book, an account, a statement, a voucher, an invoice, a letter, a telegram, an agreement and a memorandum, whether recorded in writing or in some other manner and whether or not some process must be applied to the record to make it readily intelligible;

"registrant" "registrant" means a person who is registered, or who is required to apply to be registered, under Subdivision d of Division V;

"release" "release" has the same meaning as in the *Customs Act*;

"reporting period" "reporting period" of a person means the reporting period of the person as determined under sections 245 to 251;

"residential complex" "residential complex" means
(*a*) that part of a building (including a mobile home) in which one or more residential units are located, together with
(i) that part of any common areas and other appurtenances to the building and the land immediately contiguous to the building that is reasonably necessary for the use and enjoyment of the building as a place of residence for individuals, and
(ii) that proportion of the land subjacent to the building that that part of the building is of the whole building,
(*b*) that part of a building that is
(i) the whole or part of a semidetached house, rowhouse unit, residential condominium unit or other similar premises that is, or is intended to be, a separate parcel or other division of real property owned, or intended to be owned, apart from any other unit in the building, and
(ii) a residential unit,
together with that proportion of any common areas and other appurtenances to the building and the land subjacent or immediately contiguous to the building that is attributable to the unit and that is reasonably necessary for its use and enjoyment as a place of residence for individuals, and
(*c*) the whole of a building described in paragraph (*a*), or the whole of premises described in subparagraph (*b*)(i), that is owned by or has been supplied by way of sale to an individual and that is used primarily as a place of residence of the individual, an individual related to the individual or a former spouse of the individual, together with
(i) in the case of a building described in paragraph (*a*), any appurtenances to the building, the land subjacent to the building and that part of the land immediately contiguous to the building, that are reasonably necessary for the use and enjoyment of the building, and
(ii) in the case of a premises described in subparagraph (*b*)(i), that part of any common areas and other appurtenances

to the building and the land subjacent or immediately contiguous to the building that is attributable to the unit and that is reasonably necessary for the use and enjoyment of the unit, but not including any part of a building or the land or appurtenances attributable to a building where

(*d*) the building includes a hotel, a motel, an inn, a boarding house, a lodging house or other similar premises,

(*e*) the building is not described in paragraph (*c*), and

(*f*) all or substantially all of the supplies of residential units in the building by way of lease, licence or similar arrangement are, or are expected to be, for periods of less than sixty days;

"residential unit" — "residential unit" means

(*a*) a detached house, semi-detached house, rowhouse unit, condominium unit, mobile home or apartment,

(*b*) a suite or room in a hotel, a motel, an inn, a boarding house, a lodging house or a residence for students, elderly persons, infirm persons or other individuals, or

(*c*) any other similar premises,

or that part thereof that

(*d*) is occupied by an individual as a place of residence or lodging,

(*e*) is supplied by way of lease, licence or similar arrangement for the occupancy thereof as a place of residence or lodging for individuals,

(*f*) is vacant, but was last occupied or supplied as a place of residence or lodging for individuals, or

(*g*) has never been used or occupied for any purpose, but is intended to by used as a place of residence or lodging for individuals;

"sale" — "sale", in respect of property, includes any transfer of the ownership of the property and transfer of the possession of the property under an agreement to transfer ownership of the property;

"school authority" — "school authority" means an organization or that part of an organization that operates in a province an elementary or secondary school in which it provides instruction that meets the standards of educational instruction established by the government of the province;

"segregated fund" — "segregated fund" of an insurer means a specified group of properties that is held in respect of life insurance policies all or part of the reserves for which vary in amount depending on the fair market value of the properties;

"service" — "service" means anything other than

(*a*) property,

(*b*) money, and

(*c*) anything that is supplied to an employer by a person who is or agrees to become an officer or employee of the employer in the course of or in relation to the office or employment of that person;

"short-term accommodation" — "short-term accommodation" means a residential complex or a residential unit that is supplied by way of lease, licence or similar arrangement for the purpose of its occupancy by the same individual as a place of residence or lodging, where the complex or unit is occupied by the individual for a period of less than one month;

"single unit residential complex" — "single unit residential complex" means a residential complex that does not contain more than one residential unit, but does not include a residential condominium unit;

"small supplier" — "small supplier", at any time, means a person who is at that time a small supplier under section 148;

"specified tangible personal property" — "specified tangible personal property" means property that is, or is an interest in,
(*a*) a print, an etching, a drawing, a painting, a sculpture or other similar work of art,
(*b*) jewellery,
(*c*) a rare folio, a rare manuscript or a rare book,
(*d*) a stamp,
(*e*) a coin, or
(*f*) prescribed personal property;

"substantial renovation" — "substantial renovation" of a residential complex means the renovation or alteration of a building to such an extent that all or substantially all of the building that existed immediately before the renovation or alteration was begun, other than the foundation, external walls, interior supporting walls, floors, roof and staircases, has been removed or replaced where, after completion of the renovation or alteration, the building is, or forms part of, a residential complex;

"supplier" *Version* — "supplier", in respect of a supply, means the person making the supply;

"supply" — "supply" means, subject to sections 133 and 134, the provision of property or a service in any manner, including sale, transfer, barter, exchange, licence, rental, lease, gift or disposition;

"tax" — "tax" means tax payable under this Part;

"taxable supply" — "taxable supply" means a supply that is made in the course of a commercial activity, but does not include an exempt supply;

"taxation year" — "taxation year" of a person means
(*a*) where the person is a taxpayer within the meaning of that term in the *Income Tax Act*, the taxation year of the person for the purposes of that Act, and
(*b*) in any other case, the period that would be the taxation year of the person for the purposes of that Act if the person were a corporation;

"Tax Court" — "Tax Court" means the Tax Court of Canada;

"tax fraction" — "tax fraction" means 7/107;

"university" — "university" means a recognized degree-granting institution and an organization or that part of an organization that operates a college affiliated with such an institution or that operates a research body of such an institution;

"used tangible personal property" and "used specified tangible personal property" — "used tangible personal property" means tangible personal property that has, at any time, been used in Canada and "used specified tangible personal property" means specified tangible personal property unless satisfactory evidence is available to establish that
(*a*) where the property is a print, an etching, a drawing, a painting, a sculpture or other similar work of art, it has been held in Canada solely for supply in the ordinary course of business by a registrant since the latest of
(i) the day the person ;who created the property first made a supply by way of sale of the property,
(ii) the beginning of January 1, 1991, and
(iii) the day the property was

last imported, and

(*b*) where the property is property not referred to in paragraph (*a*), it has been held in Canada solely for supply in the ordinary course of business by a registrant since the later of

(i) the beginning of January 1, 1991, and

(ii) the day the property was last imported;

"zero-rated supply" "zero-rated supply" means a supply included in Schedule VI.

PART I

REAL PROPERTY

1. In this Part, "improvement", in respect of real property of a person, means any property or service supplied to, or goods imported by, the person for the purpose of improving the real property, to the extent that the consideration paid or payable by the person for the property or service or the value of the goods is, or would be if the person were a taxpayer under the *Income Tax Act*, included in determining the cost or, in case of real property that is capital property of the person, the adjusted cost base to the person of the property for the purposes of that Act.

2. A supply by way of sale of a residential complex or an interest therein made by a person who is not the builder of the complex or, where the complex is a multiple unit residential complex, an addition thereto, unless

(*a*) the person claimed an input tax credit in respect of the acquisition of or an improvement to the complex; and

(*b*) after the person claimed the credit and before ownership of the complex or interest is transferred to the recipient of the supply, the person was not deemed to have made another supply by way of sale of the complex under subsection 206(4) or 207(1) of the Act or, by reason of section 210 of the Act, under subsection 200(2) of the Act.

3. A supply by way of sale of a residential complex or an interest therein made by the builder of the complex or, where the complex is a multiple unit residential complex, the builder of an addition thereto, if

(*a*) the builder is an individual,

(*b*) at any time after the construction or substantial renovation of the complex or addition is substantially completed, the complex is used primarily as a place of residence of the individual, an individual related to the individual or a former spouse of the individual, and

(*c*) the complex is not used primarily for any other purpose after the construction or substantial renovation is substantially completed and before that time,

Unless the individual claimed an input tax credit in respect of the acquisition of or an improvement to the complex and, after the individual claimed the credit and before ownership of the complex or interest is transferred to the recipient of the supply, the individual was not deemed under subsection 207(1) of the Act to have made another supply by way of sale of the complex.

4. A supply by way of sale of a single unit residential complex or a residential condominium unit or an interest in the complex or unit made by the builder of the complex or unit if, before ownership of the complex, unit or interest is transferred to the recipient of the supply, the builder was deemed under subsection 191(1) or (2) of the Act to have made at any time another supply of the complex unless, after that time,

(*a*) the builder claimed an input tax credit in respect of the acquisition of or an improvement to the complex or unit; and

(*b*) after the builder claimed the credit and before ownership of the complex or interest is transferred to the recipient of the supply, the builder was not deemed under subsection 206(4) or 207(1) of the Act or, by reason of section 210 of the Act, under subsection 200(2) of the Act to have made another supply by way of sale of the complex or unit.

5. A supply by way of sale of a multiple unit residential complex or an interest therein

(*a*) made by a person who is the builder of the complex if, before ownership of the complex or interest is transferred to the recipient of the supply, the builder was deemed under subsection 191(3) of the Act to have made another supply of the complex, or (*b*) made by a person who is not the builder of the complex but is the builder of an addition to the complex,

unless

(*c*) the person claimed an input tax credit in respect of the acquisition of or an improvement to the complex, other than in respect of the construction or substantial renovation of the complex or addition, and

(*d*) after the person claimed the credit and before ownership of the complex or interest is transferred to the recipient of the supply, the person was not deemed under subsection 206(4) or 207(1) of the Act or, by reason of section 210 of the Act, under subsection 200(2) of the Act to have made another supply by way of sale of the complex,

but not including that part of the supply that may reasonably be regarded as the supply of an addition to the complex, or an interest in an addition, of which

(*e*) the person is the builder, and

(*f*) the person was not deemed under subsection 191(4) of the Act to have made another supply.

6. A supply

(*a*) of a residential complex or a residential unit in a residential complex by way of lease, licence or similar arrangement for the purpose of its occupancy as a place of residence or lodging by the same individual, where it is occupied by the individual for a period of at least one month; or

(*b*) of a residential unit by way of lease, licence or similar arrangement for the purpose of its occupancy as a place of residence or lodging by the same individual, where the consideration for the supply does not exceed $20 for each day of occupancy or $140 for each week of occupancy.

6.1 A supply of real property that is

(*a*) land; or

(*b*) a building, or part of a building, where the building or such part, as the case may be, consists solely of residential units,

by way of lease, licence or similar arrangement to a particular person for a period during which the supply by the particular person, or by any other person, of the property or of all or substantially all of the parts of the land or the residential units in the property, as the case may be, is exempt under section 6 or 7 or this section.

7. A supply of land by way of lease, licence or similar arrangement made to the owner or lessee of a mobile home, or any other residential unit, affixed or to be affixed to the land where the term of the arrangement is a period of not less than one month, but not including any land contiguous to the reasonably necessary for the use and enjoyment of the unit as a place of residence for individuals.

8. A supply of a parking space, where the supply is incidental to the use of land, a residential complex or a residential unit in a residential complex, the supply of which is included in any of sections 2 to 7.

9. A supply of real property by way of sale made by an individual or a trust, all the beneficiaries of which are individuals, other than

(*a*) a supply of real property that is, immediately before the time ownership or possession of the property is transferred to the recipient of the supply under the agreement for the supply, capital property used primarily in a business of the individual or trust;

(*b*) a supply of real property made

(i) in the course of a business of the individual or trust, or

(ii) where the individual has filed an election with the Minister in the prescribed form and manner and containing the prescribed information, in the course of an adventure or concern in the nature of trade of the individual or trust that is not a business;

(*c*) a supply deemed under section 206 or 207 of the Act to have been made; or

(*d*) a supply of a residential complex.

10. A supply of farmland by way of sale made by an individual to another individual who is related to or who is a former spouse of the individual where

(*a*) the farmland was used at any time by the individual in a commercial activity that is the business of farming;

(*b*) the farmland was not used, immediately before the time ownership of the property is transferred under the supply, by the individual in a commercial activity other than the business of farming; and

(*c*) the other individual is acquiring the farmland for the personal use and enjoyment of that other individual or any individual related thereto.

11. A supply by an individual of farmland deemed under subsection 190(2) or 207(1) of the Act to have been made where

(*a*) the farmland was used at any time by the individual in a commercial activity that is the business of farming;

(*b*) the farmland was not used, immediately before the time the supply is deemed to have been made, by the individual in a commercial activity other than the business of farming; and

(*c*) the farmland is, immediately after the time the supply is deemed to have been made, for the personal use and enjoyment of the individual or an individual related thereto.

12. A supply of farmland by way of sale made to a particular individual, an individual related to the particular individual or a former spouse of the particular individual by a person that is a corporation, partnership or trust where

(*a*) immediately before the time ownership of the property is transferred under the supply,

(i) all or substantially all of the property of the person is used in a commercial activity that is the business of farming,

(ii) the particular individual is a member of the partnership, a beneficiary of the trust or a shareholder of or related to the corporation, as the case may be, and

(iii) the particular individual, the spouse of the particular individual or a child (within the meaning of paragraph 70(10)(*a*) of the *Income Tax Act*) of the particular individual is actively engaged in the business of the person; and

(*b*) immediately after the time ownership of the property is transferred under the supply, the farmland is for the personal use and enjoyment of the individual to whom the supply was made or an individual related thereto.

13. A supply made by a condominium corporation to the owner or lessee of a residential condominium unit in the condominium complex managed by the condominium corporation of property or a service relating to the occupancy or use of the unit.

14. For the purposes of sections 4 and 5, section 191 of the Act shall be deemed to have been in force at all times before 1991.

PART II

HEALTH CARE SERVICES

1. In this Part,

"health care facility" means

(*a*) a facility, or a part thereof, operated for the purpose of providing medical or hospital care, including acute, rehabilitative or chronic care,

(*b*) a hospital or institution primarily for the mentally disordered, or

(*c*) a facility, or a part thereof, operated for the purpose of providing nursing home intermediate care service or residential care service, within the meaning of the *Canada Health Act*, or comparable services for children;

"institutional health care service" means any of the following when provided in a health care facility:

(*a*) laboratory, radiological or other diagnostic services,

(*b*) drugs, biologicals or related preparations when administered in the facility in conjunction with the supply of a service included in any of paragraphs (*a*) and (*c*) to (*g*),

(*c*) the use of operating rooms, case rooms or anaesthetic facilities, including any necessary equipment or supplies

(i) used by the operator of the facility in providing a service included in any of paragraphs (*a*) to (*c*) and (*e*) to (*g*), or

(ii) supplied to a patient or resident of the facility otherwise than by way of sale,

(*e*) the use of radiotherapy, physiotherapy or occupational therapy facilities,

(*f*) accommodation,

(*g*) meals (other than meals served in a restaurant, cafeteria or similar eating establishment), and

(*h*) services rendered by persons who receive remuneration therefor from the operator of the facility;

"insured person" has the same meaning as in the *Canada Health Act*;

"medical practitioner" means a person who is entitled under the laws of a province to practise the profession of medicine or dentistry;

"practitioner", in respect of a supply of optometric, chiropractic, physiotherapy, chiropodic, podiatric, osteopathic, audiological, speech-therapy, occupational therapy, or psychological services, means a person who

(*a*) is licensed or otherwise certified to practise the profession of optometry, chiropractic, physiotherapy, chiropody, podiatry, osteopathy, audiology, speech-therapy, occupational therapy, or psychology in the province in which the service is supplied, or

(*b*) where the person is not required to be licensed or otherwise certified to practise the profession of the person in the province in which the service is supplied, has the qualifications equivalent to those necessary to be so licensed or otherwise certified in another province, and

(*c*) in respect of the supply of psychological services, is registered in the Canadian Register of Health Service Providers in Psychology,

and practises the profession of optometry, chiropractic, physiotherapy, chiropody, podiatry, osteopathy, audiology, speech-therapy, occupational therapy, or psychology, as the case may be.

2. A supply of an institutional health care service made by the operator of a health care facility to a patient or resident of the facility, but not including a service related to the provision of a surgical or dental service that is performed for cosmetic purposes and not for medical or reconstructive purposes.

3. A supply made by the operator of a health care facility by way of lease of medical equipment or supplies to consumer on the written order of medical practitioner.

4. A supply of an ambulance service made by a person who carried on the business of supplying ambulance services.

5. A supply made by a medical practitioner of a consultative, diagnostic, treatment or other health care service rendered to an individual (other than a surgical or dental service that is performed for cosmetic purposes).

6. A supply of a nursing service rendered by a registered nurse, a registered nursing assistant or a licensed practical nurse, where

(*a*) the service is rendered to an individual in a health care facility or in the individual's place of residence;

(*b*) the service is a private-duty nursing service; or

(*c*) the supply is made to a public sector body.

7. A supply of any of the following services when rendered to an individual, where the supply is made by a practitioner of the service;

(*a*) optometric services;
(*b*) chiropractic services;
(*c*) physiotherapy services;
(*d*) chiropodic services;
(*e*) podiatric services;
(*f*) osteopathic services;
(*g*) audiological services;
(*h*) speech-therapy services;
(*i*) occupational therapy services; and
(*j*) psychological services.

8. A supply of a dental hygienist service.

9. A supply of any property or service but only if, and to the extent that, the consideration for the supply is payable or reimbursed by the government of a province under a plan established under an Act of the legislature of the province to provide for health care services for all insured persons of the province.

10. A supply of a prescribed diagnostic, treatment or other health care service when made on the order of a medical practitioner or practitioner.

11. A supply of food and beverages, including the services of a caterer, made to an operator of a health care facility under a contract to provide on a regular basis meals for the patients or residents of the facility.

12. A supply of a psychoanalytic service made by a person who

(*a*) has received the same training in the provision of psychoanalytic services from the same training institute as medical practitioners who provide psychoanalytic services; and

(*b*) is a member in good standing of the professional society in respect of the provision of psychoanalytic services in Canada that

(i) sets and maintains the same standards of practice and conduct in respect of all members of the society, and

(ii) consists of at least 300 members in Canada of which at least 2/3 are medical practitioners.

PART III

EDUCATIONAL SERVICES

1. In this Part,

"elementary or secondary school student" means an individual who is enrolled in a school that is operated by a school authority in a province and in

(*a*) courses that are at the elementary level of education, or

(*b*) courses for which credit may by obtained toward a diploma or certificate issued or approved by the government of the province or courses equivalent to such courses;

"provincial regulatory body" means a body that is constituted or empowered by an Act of the legislature of a province to regulate the practice of profession or trade in the province to regulate the practice of a profession or trade in the province by setting standards of knowledge and proficiency for practitioners of the profession or trade and by registering or licensing persons to practise the profession or trade in that province;

"vocational school" means an organization that is established and operated primarily to provide students with

(*a*) correspondence courses, or

(*b*) instruction in courses

that develop or enhance students' occupational skills and includes an educational institution that is certified by the Minister of Employment and Immigration for the purposes of subsection 118.5(1) of the *Income Tax Act*.

2. A supply made by a school authority in a province of a service of instructing individuals in a course that is provided primarily for elementary or secondary school students.

3. A supply of food, beverages or services, including admissions, made by a school authority primarily to elementary or secondary school students during the course of extra-curricular activities organized under the authority and responsibility of the school authority.

4. A supply made by a school authority of a service performed by an elementary or secondary school student or by an instructor of an elementary or secondary school student in the ordinary course of the instruction of the student.

5. A supply made by a school authority to elementary or secondary school students of a service of transporting the students to or from a school that is operated by a school authority.

6. A supply of a service of instructing individuals in, or administering examinations in respect of, courses leading to, or for the purpose of maintaining or upgrading, a professional or trade accreditation or designation recognized by a provincial regulatory body, where the supply is made by a professional or trade association, government, vocational school, university or public college or by the provincial regulatory body, except where the supplier has filed with the Minister an election under this section in prescribed form containing prescribed information.

7. A supply made by a school authority, public college or university of a service of instructing individuals in, or administering examinations in respect of, courses for which credit may be obtained toward a diploma or degree.

8. A supply made by a school authority, vocational school, public college or university of a service of instructing individuals in, or administering examinations in respect of, courses leading to certificates, diplomas, licences or similar documents, or classes or ratings in respect of licences, that are prescribed by federal or provincial regulation and that attest to the competence of individuals to practise or perform a trade or vocation.

9. A supply of a service of tutoring an individual in a course that either follows a curriculum that is designated by a school authority or is a prescribed equivalent of such a course.

10. A supply of a service of instructing individual where the instruction is a prerequisite to a course that either follows a curriculum that is designated by a school authority or is a prescribed equivalent of such a course.

11. A supply of a service of instructing individuals in, or administering examinations in respect of, language courses that form part of a program of second-language instruction in either English or French, where the supply is made by a school authority, public college or university or an organization that is established and operated primarily to provide instruction in languages.

12. A supply of food or beverages (other than prescribed food or beverages or food or beverages supplied through a vending machine) where the supply is made in an elementary or secondary school cafeteria primarily to students of the school, except where the supply is for a private party, reception, meeting or similar private event.

13. A supply of a meal at a university or public college to a student where the meal is provided under a plan under which the student purchases from the supplier for a single consideration a supply of not less than 10 meals weekly for a period not less than one month.

14. A supply of food and beverages, including catering services, made to a person that is a school authority, university, or public college under a contract to provide food or beverages

(*a*) to students under a plan referred to in section 13; or

(*b*) in an elementary or secondary school cafeteria primarily to students of the school,

except to the extent that the food, beverages and services are provided for a reception, conference or other special occasion or event.

15. A supply of personal property made by way of lease by a school authority to an elementary or secondary school student.

16. A supply made by a public college or university of a service of instructing individuals in, or administering examinations in respect of, courses that are part of a program that consists of two or more courses (other than courses in sports, games, hobbies or other recreational pursuits that are designed to be taken primarily for recreational purposes) and that is subject to the review of, and is approved by, a council, board or committee of the university or college established to review and approve the course offerings of the university or college.

PART IV

CHILD AND PERSONAL CARE SERVICES

1. A supply of child care services, the primary purpose of which is to provide care and supervision to children 14 years of age or under for periods normally less than 24 hours per day.

2. A supply made by a person of a service of providing care and supervision to a resident of an institution established and operated by the person for the purpose of providing such service and of providing a place of residence for children or disabled or underprivileged individuals.

PART V

LEGAL AID SERVICES

1. A supply of legal services provided under a legal aid plan administered by or under the authority of a government of a province made by the person responsible for administering the plan.

PART VI

PUBLIC SECTOR BODIES

1. In this Part,

"direct cost" of a film, slide show or similar presentation or of supply of tangible personal property or service means the total of all amounts each of which is the value of consideration paid or payable by the supplier

(*a*) of admissions in respect of the presentation, or

(*b*) of the property or service,

for an article or material (other than capital property of the supplier) that was purchased by the supplier, to the extent that the article or material is to be incorporated into or is to form a constituent or component part of the property or is to be consumed or expended directly in staging the presentation, supplying the service or in the process of manufacturing, producing, processing or packaging the property, and includes

(*c*) in the case of supply of property or a service that was previously purchased by the supplier, the value of consideration paid or payable by the supplier for the property or service, and

(*d*) in the case of a film, slide show or similar presentation, the total of all amounts each of which is the value of consideration paid or payable by the supplier of admissions in respect of the presentation for the rental of, or right to use, any film, slide or similar property or projector or similar equipment used for the presentation,

and, for the purposes of this definition, the consideration paid or payable by a supplier for property or a service shall be deemed to include the amount, if any, by which the tax payable by the supplier in respect of the property or service exceeds the total of all amounts each of which is an input tax credit of the supplier or a rebate under Part IX of the Act that the supplier has claimed or is entitled to claim in respect of the property or service;

"homemaker service" means a household or personal service, such as cleaning, laundering, meal preparation and child care, that is provided to an individual who, due to age, infirmity or disability, requires assistance;

"municipal transit service" means a public passenger transportation service (other than a charter service or a service that is part of a tour) that is supplied by a transit authority all or substantially all of whose supplies are of public passenger transportation services provided within a particular municipality and its environs;

"transit authority" means

(*a*) a division, department or agency of a government, municipality or school authority, the primary purpose of which is to supply public passenger transportation services, or

(*b*) a non-profit organization that

(i) receives funding from a government, municipality or school authority to support the supply of public passenger transportation services to disabled individuals.

2. A supply made by a charity of any personal property or a service, but not including a supply of

(*a*) property or a service included in Schedule VI and not included in section 6 or 10;

(*b*) property or a service the supply of which is deemed under Part IX of the Act to have been made by the charity;

(*c*) property (other than capital property of the charity or property that was acquired, manufactured or produced by the charity for the purpose of making a supply of the property) where, immediately before the time tax would be payable in respect of the supply if it were a taxable supply, the property was used (otherwise than in making the supply) in commercial activities of the charity;

(*d*) capital property of the charity where, immediately before the time tax would be payable in respect of the supply if it were a taxable supply, the property was used (otherwise than in making the supply) primarily in commercial activities of the charity;

(*e*) tangible property that was acquired, manufactured or produced by the charity for the purpose of making a supply of the property and was neither donated to the charity nor used by another person before its acquisition by the charity, or any service supplied by the charity in respect of such property, other than such property or such a service supplied by the charity under a contract for catering;

(*f*) property made by way of lease, licence or similar arrangement in conjunction with a supply of real property included in paragraph 25(*f*);

(*g*) property or a service made by the charity under a contract for catering for an event or occasion sponsored or arranged by another person who contracts with the charity for catering;

(*h*) an admission in respect of a place of amusement or a membership where the membership

(i) entitles entitles the member to supplies of admissions in respect of a place of amusement that would be taxable supplies if they were made separately from the supply of the membership, or to discounts on the value of consideration for such supplies, or

(ii) includes a right to participate in a recreational or athletic activity, or use facilities, at a place of amusement,

except where the value of the supplies, discounts or right described in subparagraph (i) or (ii) is insignificant in relation to the consideration for the membership;

(*i*) services of performing artists in a performance where the supply is made to a person who makes taxable supplies of admissions in respect of the performance;

(*j*) a service involving, or a membership or other right entitling a person to, supervision or instruction in any recreational or athletic activity;

(*k*) a right to play or participate in a game of chance;

(*l*) a service of instructing individuals in, or administering examinations in respect of, any course where the supply is made by a vocational school, as defined in section 1 of Part III, or a school authority, public college or university; or

(*m*) an admission in respect of a seminar, conference or similar event supplied by a university or public college.

3. A supply made by a charity of any property or service where

(*a*) the supply is made in the course of a business of making supplies of such property or such a service or of similar property or services carried on by the charity, and the day-to-day administrative functions and other functions performed in carrying on the business are performed exclusively by volunteers,

(*b*) the supply is made in the course of an activity engaged in by the charity otherwise than in the course of, or as part of, a business referred to in paragraph (*a*), and the day-to-day administrative functions and other functions performed in carrying on the activity, including the provision of any property or service in the course of the activity, are performed exclusively by volunteers, or

(*c*) the property or service is, and is represented to prospective recipients to be, supplied as part of a program established by the charity that consists of a series of classes or other activities and the non-administrative functions performed in providing the activities are performed exclusively by volunteers,

but not including a supply of

(*d*) property or a service included in paragraph 2(*a*), (*b*), (*c*), (*d*) or (*k*),

(*e*) an admission in respect of a place of amusement at which bets are placed or a game of chance is conducted, or

(*f*) real property made by way of sale.

4. A supply of tangible personal property (other than alcoholic beverages or tobacco products) made by way of sale by public sector body where

(*a*) the body does not carry on the business of selling such property;

(*b*) all the salespersons are volunteers;

(*c*) the consideration for each item sold does not exceed $5; and

(*d*) the property is not sold at an event at which supplies of property of the kind or class supplied are made by persons who carry on the business of selling such property.

5. A supply made by a public sector body of an admission in respect of a place of amusement at which the principal activity is the placing of bets or the playing of games of chance, where

(*a*) the administrative functions and other functions performed in operating the game and taking the bets are performed exclusively by volunteers; and

(*b*) in the case of a bingo or casino, the game is not conducted in premises or at a place, including any temporary structure, that is used primarily for the purposes of conducting gambling activities.

5.1 A supply made by a charity or non-profit organization (other than a prescribed person) of a right to play or participate in a game of chance (other than a prescribed game of chance).

5.2 A supply of a service that is deemed under section 187 of the Act to have been supplied

(*a*) by a charity or non-profit organization (other than a prescribed person); or

(*b*) where the service is in respect of a bet made through the agency of a pari-mutuel system on a running, trotting or pacing horse-race.

6. A supply made by a public service body of

(*a*) a service, where the supply is made in the course of a business of making supplies of the service, or

(*b*) tangible personal property,

where the value of the consideration for the supply paid or payable by the recipient is equal to the usual charge by the body for such supplies to such recipients and does not, or could not reasonably be expected to, exceed the direct cost of the supply.

7. A supply of any service, other than a supply included in section 6, made by a public service body in the course of an event or activity, where the total of all amounts, each of which is the consideration for a supply of such a service made by the body in the course of that event or activity, could not reasonably be expected to exceed the aggregate of all amounts each of which is the direct cost of supply of such a service made by the body in the course of that event or activity.

8. A supply made by a public sector body of an admission in respect of a film, slide show or similar presentation where the total of all amounts, each of which is the consideration for an admission in respect of the presentation could not reasonably be expected to exceed the direct cost of the presentation.

9. A supply made at any time by a public sector body of an admission in respect of a place of amusement where the maximum consideration for a supply at that time by the body of an admission in respect of the place does not exceed one dollar.

10. A supply made by a public sector body of any property or service where all or substantially all of the supplies of the property or service by the body are made for no consideration.

11. A supply of a right to be a spectator at a performance, athletic event or competitive event, where all or substantially all of the performers, ath-

letes or competitors taking part in the performance or event do not receive, directly or indirectly, remuneration for doing so (other than a reasonable amount as prizes, gifts or compensation for travel or other expenses incidental to the performers', athletes' or competitors' participation in the performance or event, or grants paid by a government or a municipality to the performers, athletes or competitors), and no advertisement or representation in respect of the performance or event features participants who are so remunerated, but does not include a supply of a right to be a spectator at a competitive event in which cash prizes are awarded and in which any competitor is a professional participant in any competitive event.

12. A supply made by a public sector body of a membership in, or services supplied as part of, a program established and operated by the body that consists of a series of supervised instructional classes or activities involving athletics, outdoor recreation, music, dance, arts, crafts or other hobbies or recreational pursuits where

(*a*) it may reasonably be expected, given the nature of the classes or activities or the degree of relevant skill or ability required for participation in them, that the program will be provided primarily to children 14 years of age or under, except where the program involves overnight supervision throughout a substantial portion of the program; or

(*b*) the program is provided primarily for underprivileged or mentally or physically disabled individuals.

13. A supply made by a public sector body of board and lodging or recreational services at a recreational camp or similar place under a program or arrangement for providing the board and lodging or services primarily to underprivileged or mentally or physically disabled individuals.

14. A supply made by a public sector body of food, beverages or short-term accommodation where the supply is made in the course of an activity the purpose of which is to relieve poverty, suffering or distress of individuals and is not fund-raising.

15. A supply made by a public sector body of food or beverages to aged, infirm, disabled or underprivileged individuals under a program established and operated for the purpose of providing prepared food to those individuals in their places of residence and any supply of food or beverages made to the public sector body for the purpose of the program.

16. A supply of a homemaker service that is provided to an individual in the individual's place of residence, where the supply is made by

(*a*) a government or municipality; or

(*b*) a non-profit organization that receives an amount paid by a government or municipality in respect of the supply.

17. A supply of a membership in a public sector body (other than a membership in a club the main purpose of which is to provide dining, recreational or sporting facilities) where each member does not receive a benefit by reason of the membership, other than

(*a*) an indirect benefit that is intended to accrue to all members collectively,

(*b*) the right to receive services supplied by the body that are in the nature of investigating, conciliating or settling complaints or disputes involving members,

(*c*) the right to vote at or participate in meetings,

(*d*) the right to receive or acquire property or services supplied to the member for consideration that is not part of the consideration for the membership and that is equal to the fair market value of the property or services at the time the supply is made,

(*e*) the right to receive a discount on the value of the consideration for a supply to be made by the body where the total value of all such discounts to which a member is entitled by reason of the membership is insignificant in relation to the consideration for the membership, or

(*f*) the right to receive periodic newsletters, reports or publications

(i) the value of which is insignificant in relation to the consideration for the membership, or

(ii) that provide information on the activities of the body or its financial status, other than newsletters, reports or publications the value of which is significant in relation to the consideration for the membership and for which a fee is ordinarily charged by the body to non-members,

except where the body has filed with the Minister an election under this section in prescribed form containing prescribed information.

18. A supply of a membership made by an organization membership in which is required to maintain a professional status recognized by statute, except

where the supplier has filed with the Minister an election under this section in prescribed form containing prescribed information.

19. A supply made by a public sector body of a right that confers borrowing privileges at a public lending library.

20. The following supplies made by a government or municipality or by a board, commission or other body established by a government or municipality:

(*a*) a supply of service of registering any property or filing any document in a property registration system,

(*b*) a supply of service of the filing or procuring of a document in a court,

(*c*) a supply of a licence, permit, quota or similar right (other than such a right supplied in respect of the importation of alcoholic beverages),

(*d*) a supply of a service of providing information in respect of, or of any certificate or other document evidencing, the vital statistics, residency, citizenship or right to vote of any person, the registration of any person for any service provided by the government or any other status of any person,

(*e*) a supply of

(i) a service of providing information in respect of, or

(ii) any certificate or other document evidencing, the title to, any right or estate in, or any encumbrance in respect of, property,

(*f*) a supply of a service of providing information under the *Access to Information Act*,

(*g*) a supply of law enforcement service or a fire protection service made to a government or a municipality or to a board, commission or other body established by a government or municipality,

(*h*) a supply of garbage collection services, but not including a supply of a service that is not part of the basic garbage collection service supplied by the government or municipality on a regularly scheduled basis, and

(*i*) a supply of a right to deposit refuse at a refuse disposal site,

but not including

(*j*) a supply to a consumer of a right to hunt or fish,

(*k*) a supply of a right to take or remove minerals, forestry products, water or fishery products, where the right is supplied to

(i) a consumer, or

(ii) a person who is not a registrant and who acquires the right in the course of a business of making supplies of the minerals, forestry products, water or fishery products to consumers, or

(*l*) a supply of a right to enter, to have access to or to use property of the government, municipality or other body.

21. A supply of municipal service made by or on behalf of a government or municipality to owners or occupants of real property situated in particular geographic area where the owners or occupants have no option but to receive the service, other than a supply of a service of testing or inspecting any property for the purpose of verifying or certifying that the property meets particular standards of quality or is suitable for consumption, use or supply in a particular manner.

22. A supply of a service made by or on behalf of a government or municipality, or by an organization designated by the Minister to be a municipality for the purposes of this section, of installing, repairing or maintaining a water distribution, sewerage or drainage system that is for the use of all occupants and owners of real property situated in a particular geographic area, but not including a supply of a service for which a separate charge is made to the recipient of repairing or maintaining any part of the system that is for the sole use of the occupants or owners of a particular parcel of real property.

23. A supply of unbottled water made by a government, municipality or designated organization referred to in section 22.

24. A supply of municipal transit service or a public passenger transportation service designated by the Minister to be a municipal transit service.

25. A supply or real property made by a public service body (other than a financial institution or a government), but not including a supply of

(*a*) a residential complex or an interest therein made by way of sale;

(*b*) real property where the supply is deemed under Part IX of the Act to have been made;

(*c*) real property made by way of sale to an individual, other than a supply of real property on which is situated a structure that was used by the body

(i) as an office, or

(ii) in the curse of commercial activities or of making exempt supplies;

(*d*) real property where, immediately before the time tax would be payable in respect of the supply if it were a taxable supply, the property was used (otherwise than in making the supply) primarily in commercial activities of the body;

(*e*) short-term accommodation made by a non-profit organization, municipality, university, public college or school authority;

(*f*) real property (other than short-term accommodation) made by way of lease, licence or similar arrangement for a period of less than one month, where the supply is made in the course of a business carried on by the body;

(*g*) real property in respect of which an election under section 211 of the Act is in effect at the time tax would become payable under Part IX of the Act in respect of the supply if it were a taxable supply; or

(*h*) a parking space made by way of lease, licence or similar arrangement in the course of a business carried on by the body.

26. A supply made by a particular non-profit organization established primarily for the benefit of organized labour where the supply is made to

(*a*) a trade union, association or body referred to in paragraphs 189(*a*) to (*c*) of the Act that is a member of or affiliated with the organization, or

(*b*) another non-profit organization established primarily for the benefit of organized labour,

or a supply made by a person referred to in paragraph (*a*) or (*b*) to any such organization.

PART VII

FINANCIAL SERVICES

1. A supply of a financial service that is not included in Part IX of Schedule VI.

2. A supply deemed under subsection 150(1) of the Act to be a supply of a financial service.

PART VIII

FERRY, ROAD AND BRIDGE TOLLS

1. A supply of a service of ferrying by watercraft passengers or property where the principal purpose of the ferrying is to transport motor vehicles and passengers between parts of a road or highway system that are separated by a stretch of water.

2. A supply of a right to use a road or bridge where a toll is charged for the right.

SCHEDULE VI

(Subsection 123(1))

ZERO-RATED SUPPLIES

PART 1

PRESCRIPTION DRUGS

1. In this Part,

"pharmacist" means a person who is entitled under the laws of a province to practise the profession of pharmacy;

"practitioner" means a person who is entitled under the laws of a province to practise the profession of medicine or dentistry;

"prescription" means a written or verbal order, given to a pharmacist by a practitioner, directing that a stated amount of any drug or mixture of drugs specified in the order be dispensed for the individual named in the order.

2. A supply of any of the following:

(*a*) a drug described in Schedule D to the *Food and Drugs Act*,

(*b*) a drug described in Schedule F to the *Food and Drug Regulations*, other than a drug or mixture of drugs that may be sold to a consumer without a prescription pursuant to the *Food and Drugs Act* or those Regulations,

(*c*) a drug or other substance included in Schedule G to the *Food and Drugs Act*,

(*d*) a drug that contains a substance included in the schedule to the *Narcotic Control Act*, other than a drug or mixture of drugs that may be sold to a consumer without a prescription pursuant to that Act or regulations made under that Act, and

(*e*) any of the following drugs, namely,

(i) Digoxin,
(ii) Digitoxin,
(iii) Prenylamine,
(iv) Deslanoside,
(v) Erythrityl tetranitrate,
(vi) Isosorbide dinitrate,
(vii) Nitroglycerine,
(viii) Quinidine and its salts,
(ix) Medical oxygen, and
(x) Epinephrine and its salts,

but not including a supply of a drug when it is labelled or supplied for agricultural or veterinary use only.

3. A supply of a drug when the drug is for human use and is dispensed

(*a*) by a practitioner to an individual for the personal consumption or use of the individual or an individual related thereto; or

(*b*) on the prescription of a practitioner for the personal consumption or use of the individual named in the prescription.

4. A supply of a service of dispensing a drug where the supply of the drug is included in this Part.

Part II

Medical Devices

1. In this Part,

"cosmetic" means a property, whether or not possessing therapeutic or prophylactic properties, commonly or commercially known as a toilet article, preparation or cosmetic that is intended for use or application for toilet purposes or for use in connection with the care of the human body, or any part thereof, whether for cleansing, deodorizing, beautifying, preserving or restoring, and includes a toilet soap, skin cream or lotion, mouth wash, oral rinse, toothpaste, tooth powder, denture cream or adhesive, antiseptic, bleach, depilatory, perfume, scent and any similar toilet article, preparation or cosmetic;

"practitioner" means a person who is entitled under the laws of a province to practise the profession of medicine.

2. A supply of a communication device for use with telegraph or telephone apparatus by an individual with a hearing or speech impairment when the device is supplied on the written order of a practitioner.

3. A supply of a heart-monitoring device when the device is supplied to a consumer on the written order of a practitioner for use by an incapacitated individual.

5. A supply of an artificial breathing apparatus that is specially designed for use by an individual with a respiratory disorder.

6. A supply of a mechanical percussor for postural drainage treatment.

7. A supply of a device that is designed to convert sound to light signals when the device is supplied on the written order of a practitioner for use by an individual with a hearing impairment.

8. A supply of a selector control device that is specially designed for use by a physically disabled individual to enable the individual to select, energize or control household, industrial or office equipment.

9. A supply of eyeglasses or contact lenses when the eyeglasses or lenses are supplied for the treatment or correction of a defect of vision to a consumer on the written order of an eye-care professional who is entitled under the laws of the province in which the professional practises to prescribe eyeglasses or contact lenses for that purpose.

10. A supply of an artificial eye.

11. A supply of artificial teeth.

12. A supply of hearing aid.

13. A supply of a laryngeal speaking aid.

14. A supply of an invalid chair, commode chair, walker, wheelchair lift or similar aid to locomotion, with or without wheels, including motive power and wheel assemblies therefor, that is specially designed for use by a disabled individual.

15. A supply of a patient lifter that is specially designed to move a disabled individual.

16. A supply of a wheelchair ramp that is specially designed for access to a motor vehicle.

17. A supply of a portable wheelchair ramp.

18. A supply of an auxiliary driving control that is designed for attachment to a motor vehicle to facilitate the operation of the vehicle by a physically disabled individual.

19. A supply of patterning device that is specially designed for use by a disabled individual.

20. A supply of a toilet-, bath- or shower-seat that is specially designed for use by a disabled individual.

21. A supply of an insulin infusion pump or an insulin syringe.

22. A supply of an artificial limb.

23. A supply of spinal or other orthopaedic brace.

24. A supply of a specially constructed appliance that is made to order for an individual who has a crippled or deformed foot or ankle.

25. A supply of medical or surgical prosthesis, or an ileostomy, colostomy or urinary appliance or similar article that is designed to be worn by an individual.

26. A supply of an article or material, not including a cosmetic, for use by a user of, and necessary for the proper application and maintenance of, a prosthesis, appliance or similar article described in section 25.

27. A supply of a cane or crutch that is designed for use by a physically disabled individual.

28. A supply of a blood-glucose monitor or meter.

29. A supply of blood-sugar testing strips, blood-ketone testing strips, urinary-sugar testing strips, reagents or tablets, or urinary-keytone testing strips, reagents or tablets.

30. A supply of any article that is specially designed for the use of blind individuals when the article is supplied for use by a blind individual to, by or on the order or certificate of a practitioner, the Canadian National Institute for the Blind or any other bona fide institution or association for the blind.

31. A supply of a prescribed property or service.

32. A supply of a part, accessory or attachment that is specially designed for a property described in this Part.

33. A supply of a dog that is or is to be trained as a guide dog for the use of a blind individual, including the service of training the individual to use the dog, where the supply is made to or by an organization that is operated for the purpose of supplying guide dogs to blind individuals.

34. A supply of a service, other than a service the supply of which is included in Part II of Schedule V, of installing, maintaining, restoring, repairing or modifying a property described in any of sections 2 to 23 of this Part, or any part for such a property where the part is supplied in conjunction with the service.

Part III

Basic Groceries

1. Supplies of food or beverages for human consumption (including sweetening agents, seasonings and other ingredients to be mixed with or used in the preparation of such food or beverages), other than supplies of

(*a*) wine, spirits, beer, malt liquor or other alcoholic beverages;

(*b*) non-alcoholic malt beverages;

(*c*) carbonated beverages;

(*d*) non-carbonated fruit juice beverages or fruit flavoured beverages, other than milk-based beverages, that contain less than 25% by volume of

(i) a natural fruit juice or combination of natural fruit juices, or

(ii) a natural fruit juice or combination of natural fruit juices that have been reconstituted into the original state,

or goods that, when added to water, produce a beverage included in the paragraph;

(*e*) candies, confectionery that may be classed as candy, or any goods sold as candies, such as candy floss, chewing gum and chocolate, whether naturally or artificially sweetened, and including fruits, seeds, nuts and popcorn when they are coated or treated with candy, chocolate, honey, molasses, sugar, syrup or artificial sweeteners;

(*f*) chips, crisps, puffs, curls or sticks (such as potato chips, corn chips, cheese puffs, potato sticks, bacon crisps and cheese curls), other similar snack foods or popcorn and brittle pretzels, but not including any products than is sold primarily as a breakfast cereal;

(*g*) salted nuts or salted seeds;

(*h*) granola products, but not including any product that is sold primarily as a breakfast cereal;

(*i*) snack mixtures that contain cereals, nuts seeds, dried fruit or any other edible product, but not including any mixture that is sold primarily as a breakfast cereal;

(*j*) ice lollies or flavoured, coloured or sweetened ice waters, whether frozen or not;

(*k*) ice cream, ice milk, sherbet, frozen yoghurt or frozen pudding, or any product that contains any of those products, when packaged in single servings;

(*l*) fruit bars, rolls or drops or similar fruit-based snack foods;

(*m*) cakes, muffins, pies, pastries, tarts, cookies, doughnuts, brownies, croissants with sweetened filling or coating, or similar products where

(i) they are prepackaged for sale to consumers in quantities of less than six items each of which is a single serving, or

(ii) they are not prepackaged for sale to consumers and are sold as single servings in quantities of less than six,

but not including bread products, such as bagels, English muffins, croissants or bread rolls, without sweetened filling or coating;

(*n*) yoghurt, pudding or beverages (other than unflavoured milk), other than when packaged for

sale to consumers in multiples of single servings or in quantity exceeding a single serving or when prepared and packaged specially for consumption by babies;
(*o*) the following prepared foods and beverages sold in a form suitable for immediate consumption, either where sold or elsewhere, namely,
(i) food or beverages heated for consumption,
(ii) prepared salads,
(iii) sandwiches and similar products,
(iv) platters of cheese, cold cuts, fruit or vegetables and other arrangements of prepared food,
(v) ice cream, ice milk, sherbet, frozen yoghurt, frozen pudding or product containing any of those products when sold in single servings and dispensed at the place where it is sold, and
(vi) beverages dispensed at the place where they are sold;
(*p*) food or beverages sold through a vending machine, and
(*q*) food or beverages when sold at an establishment at which all or substantially all of the sales of food or beverages are sales of food or beverages included in any of paragraphs (*a*) to (*p*) except where
(i) the food or beverage is sold in a form not suitable for immediate consumption, having regard to the nature of the product, the quantity sold or its packaging, or
(*A*) the product is prepackaged for sale to consumers in quantities of more than five items each of which is a single serving, or
(*B*) the product is not prepackaged for sale to consumers and is sold as single servings in quantities of more than five,
and is not sold for consumption at the establishment.

PART IV

AGRICULTURE AND FISHING

1. A supply of farm livestock, poultry or bees that are ordinarily raised or kept to produce or be used as food for human consumption or to produce wool.

2. A supply of grains or seeds in their natural state or treated for seeding purposes, hay, silage or other fodder crops, that are ordinarily used as or to produce food for human consumption or feed for farm livestock or poultry, when supplied in a quantity that is larger than the quantity that is ordinarily sold or offered for sale to consumers, but not including grains, seeds or grain or seed mixtures that are packaged, prepared or sold for use as feed for wild birds or as pet food.

3. A supply of hops, barley, flax seed, straw, sugar cane or sugar beets.

4. A supply of poultry or fish eggs that are produced for hatching purposes.

5. A supply of fertilizer when supplied in bulk quantities exceeding 500 kg.

6. A supply of wool, not further processed than dried and sorted.

7. A supply of tobacco leaves, not further processed than dried and sorted.

8. A supply of fish or other marine or freshwater animals not further processed than frozen, salted, smoked, dried, scaled, eviscerated or filleted, other than any such animal that is
(*a*) not ordinarily used as food for human consumption; or
(*b*) sold as bait in recreational fishing.

9. A supply made to registrant of farmland by way of lease, licence or similar arrangement, to the extent that the consideration for the supply is a share of the production from the farmland of property the supply of which is a zero-rated supply.

10. A supply of prescribed property.

PART V

EXPORTS

1. A supply of tangible personal property (other than an excisable good) made by a person to a recipient (other than a consumer) who intends to export the property where
(*a*) the recipient exports the property as soon after the property is delivered by the person to the recipient as is reasonable having regard to the circumstances surrounding the exportation and, where applicable, to the normal business practice or the recipient;
(*b*) the property is not acquired by the recipient for the consumption, use or supply in Canada before the exportation of the property by the recipient;
(*c*) after the supply is made and before the recipient exports the property, the property is not further processed, transformed or altered in Canada ex-

cept to the extent reasonably necessary or incidental to its transportation;

(*d*) the person maintains evidence satisfactory to the Minister of the exportation of the property by the recipient; and

(*e*) the property is not transported in Canada by the recipient by means of a truck or other highway motor vehicle (other than a truck or other motor vehicle operated by a common carrier) after the property is delivered to the recipient in Canada.

2. A supply of property or service (other than a supply of real property by way of sale) made to a non-resident person who is not registered under Subdivision d of Division V of Part IX of the Act at the time the supply is made, where the property or service is acquired by the person for consumption, use or supply

(*a*) where the person carries on the business of transporting passengers or property to or from Canada by ship, aircraft or railway, in the course of so transporting passengers or property;

(*b*) in the course of operating a ship or aircraft by or on behalf of a government of a country other than Canada; or

(*c*) in the course of operating a ship for the laying or repairing of oceanic telegraph cables.

3. A supply of an excisable good where the recipient exports the good in bond.

4. A supply of a service (other than a transportation service) in respect of tangible personal property that is ordinarily situated outside Canada, that is temporarily imported for the sole purpose of having the service performed and that is exported as soon as is practicable after the service is performed.

5. A supply made to a non-resident person of a service of acting as an agent of that person, to the extent that the service is in respect of

(*a*) a supply to that person that is included in any other section of this Part; or

(*b*) a supply made outside Canada by or to that person.

6. A supply made by a person to a non-resident recipient of an emergency repair service, and of any property supplied in conjunction with such a service, in respect of a conveyance or cargo container that is being used by the person in a business of transporting passengers or goods.

7. A supply of a service made to a particular non-resident person, other than an individual, or to a non-resident individual who is outside Canada throughout the time the service is performed, but not including a supply of

(*a*) a service (other than an advisory, consulting or professional service) that is primarily for the consumption, use or enjoyment in Canada of any person or that is a postal service, other than a supply of a service in respect of a telecommunication or postal service where the supply is made by a registrant who carries on the business of supplying telecommunication or postal services to a non-resident person who is not a registrant and who carries on such a business;

(*b*) a service in respect of real property that is ordinarily situated in Canada;

(*c*) a service in respect of tangible personal property that is ordinarily situated in Canada or that is to be delivered in Canada;

(*d*) a service of acting as an agent of the non-resident individual or particular person; or

(*e*) a transportation service.

8. A supply of a service of advertising made to a non-resident person who is not registered under Subdivision d of Division V of Part IX of the Act at the time the service is performed.

9. A supply made to a non-resident person of an advisory, consulting or research service that is intended to assist the person in taking up residence or establishing a business venture in Canada.

10. A supply of an invention, patent, trade secret, trade-mark, trade-name, copyright, industrial design or other intellectual property or any right, licence or privilege to use any such property, where the recipient is a non-resident person who is not registered under Subdivision d of Division V of Part IX of the Act at the time the supply is made.

11. A supply of tangible personal property made by a person operating a duty free shop licensed as such under the Customs Act to an individual at a duty free shop for export by the individual.

12. A supply of tangible personal property made by a person to recipient where the person delivers the property to a common carrier, or mails the property, for export and delivery to the recipient at a place outside Canada.

13. A supply to a non-resident person who is not registered under Subdivision d of Division V of Part IX of the Act of services performed in respect of tangible personal property pursuant to a warranty provided by the non-resident person.

PART VI

TRAVEL SERVICES

1 A supply of the part of a tour package that is not the taxable portion of the package.

PART VII

TRANSPORTATION SERVICES

1. (1) In this Part,

"carrier" means a person who supplies a freight transportation service;

"continuous freight movement" means the transportation of tangible personal property by one or more carriers to a destination specified by the shipper of the property, where all freight transportation services supplied by the carriers are supplied as a consequence of instructions given by the shipper of the property;

"continuous journey" of an individual or a group of individuals means the set of all passenger transportation services provided to the individual or group

(*a*) and for which a single ticket or voucher in respect of all the services is issued, or

(*b*) where 2 or more tickets or vouchers are issued in respect of 2 or more legs of a single journey of the individual or group on which there is no stopover between any of the legs of the journey for which separate tickets or vouchers are issued, and all the tickets or vouchers are issued by the same supplier or by 2 or more suppliers through one agent acting on behalf of all the suppliers where

(i) all such tickets are supplied at the same time and evidence satisfactory to the Minister is maintained by the supplier or agent that there is no stopover between any of the legs of the journey for which separate tickets or vouchers are issued, or

(ii) the tickets or vouchers are issued at different times and evidence satisfactory to the Minister is submitted by the supplier or agent that there is no stopover between any of the legs of the journey for which separate tickets or vouchers are issued;

"continuous outbound freight movement" means the transfers possession of the property to a carrier and before the property is exported, it is not further processed, transformed or altered in Canada, except to the extent that is reasonably necessary for its transportation;

"destination", in respect of a continuous freight movement of property, means a place specified by the shipper of the property where possession of the property is transferred to the person to whom the property is consigned or addressed by the shipper;

"freight transportation service" means a particular service of transporting tangible personal property and, for greater certainty, includes

(*a*) a service of delivering mail, and

(*b*) any other property or service supplied to the recipient of the particular service by the person who supplies the particular service, where the other property or service is part of or incidental to the particular service, whether there is a separate charge for the other property or service,

but does not include a service provided by the supplier of a passenger transportation service of transporting an individual's baggage in connection with the passenger transportation service;

"international freight" means any flight of an aircraft, other than a flight originating and terminating in Canada, that is operated by a person in the course of a business of supplying passenger air transportation services;

"origin" means

(*a*) in respect of a continuous freight movement, the place where the first carrier that engaged in the continuous freight movement takes possession of the property being transported, and

(*b*) in respect of a continuous journey, the place where the passenger transportation service that is included in the continuous journey and that is first provided begins;

"place outside Canada", in respect of a freight transportation service, includes at a particular time a place in Canada if, at that time, the property being transported has been imported but has not been released and the property is being transported in compliance with the *Customs Act* or any other Act of Parliament that prohibits, controls or regulates the importation of goods;

"shipper" of tangible personal property means the person who, in respect of a continuous freight movement or a continuous outbound freight movement, transfers possession of the property being shipped to a carrier at the origin of the freight movement and, for greater certainty, does not include a person who is a carrier of the property to which the freight movement relates;

"stopover", in respect of a continuous journey of an individual or a group of individuals, means any place at which the individual or group embarks or disembarks a conveyance used in the provision of a passenger transportation service included in the continuous journey, for any reason other than transferring to another conveyance or to allow for servicing or refueling of the conveyance;

"taxation area" means Canada, the United States (except Hawaii) and the islands of St. Pierre and Miquelon;

"termination" of a continuous journey means the place where the passenger transportation service that is included in the continuous journey and that is last provided ends.

(2) For the purposes of this Part, where in respect of a continuous freight movement several carriers supply freight transportation services in the course of the continuous freight movement, and the shipper or the consignee of the property is, under the contract of carriage for the continuous freight movement, required to pay a particular carrier that is one of those carriers a particular amount that is part or all of the consideration for the freight transportation services supplied by those several carriers,

(*a*) the particular carrier shall be deemed to have made a supply of a freight transportation service to the shipper or consignee, as the case may be, for consideration equal to the particular amount, whether the particular amount includes an amount paid to the particular carrier as agent of any of the other several carriers;

(*b*) the shipper or consignee, as the case may be, shall be deemed to have received a supply of a freight transportation service from the particular carrier for consideration equal to the particular amount and not to have received a freight transportation service from any of the other several carriers; and

(*c*) to the extent that any part of the particular amount is paid by one of the several carriers (in this paragraph referred to as the "first carrier") to another of the several carriers, the first carrier shall be deemed to be the recipient of freight transportation services supplied by the other carriers in relation to the continuous freight movement and, to the same extent, the other carriers shall be deemed to have supplied those freight transportation services to the first carrier and not to the shipper or consignee.

2. A supply of passenger transportation service that is provided to an individual or a group of individuals and that is part of a continuous journey of the individual or group, other than a continuous journey that includes transportation by air, where

(*a*) the origin or termination of the continuous journey is outside Canada, or

(*b*) there is a stopover outside Canada,

but not including a passenger transportation service that is part of a continuous journey if both the origin and the termination of the journey are in Canada and, at the time the journey begins, the individual or group is not scheduled to be outside Canada for an uninterrupted period of at least 24 hours during the course of the journey.

3. A supply of a passenger transportation service that is provided to an individual or group of individuals and that is part of a continuous journey of the individual or group that includes transportation by air, where

(*a*) the origin or termination of the continuous journey, or any stopover in respect thereof, is outside the taxation area;

(*b*) the origin and termination of the continuous journey, and all stopovers in respect thereof, are outside Canada;

(*c*) the origin of the continuous journey is within the taxation area, but outside Canada, and the recipient of the supply tenders the consideration for the supply at a place outside Canada; or

(*d*) all places at which the individual or group embarks or disembarks an aircraft are outside Canada and the origin or termination of the continuous journey, or any stopover in respect thereof, is outside Canada.

4. A supply of a service of transporting an individual's baggage in connection with a passenger transportation service that is included in section 2 or 3 for consideration that is not included as part of the consideration for the passenger transportation ser-

vice, where the supply is made by the supplier of the passenger transportation service.

5. A supply of tangible personal property or a service made by a person, in the course of a business of making supplies of passenger transportation services, to an individual aboard an aircraft on an international flight, where the property is delivered, or the service is wholly provided, aboard the aircraft.

6. A supply of a freight transportation service in respect of the transportation of tangible personal property form a place in Canada to a place outside Canada where the value of the consideration for the supply is $5 or more.

7. A supply made by a carrier of a freight transportation service in respect of the transportation of tangible personal property from a place in Canada to another place in Canada, where

(*a*) the shipper of the property provides the carrier with a declaration in prescribed form that the property is being shipped for export and that the freight transportation service to be supplied by the carrier is part of a continuous outbound freight movement in respect of the property;

(*b*) the property is exported and the service is part of a continuous outbound freight movement in respect of the property; and

(*c*) the value of the consideration for the supply is $5 or more.

8. A supply of a freight transportation of tangible personal property from a place outside Canada to a place in Canada.

9. A supply of a freight transportation service in respect of the transportation of tangible personal property from a place outside Canada to a place in Canada.

10. A supply of a particular freight transportation service from a place in Canada to another place in Canada that is part of a continuous freight movement form an origin outside Canada to a destination in Canada, where the supplier of the service maintains documentary evidence satisfactory to the Minister that the service is part of a continuous freight movement form an origin outside Canada to a destination in Canada.

11. A supply of a freight transportation service made by a carrier of the property being transported to a second carrier of the property being transported, where the service is part of a continuous freight movement and the second carrier is neither the shipper nor the consignee of the property being transported.

12. A supply of a service of acting as an agent for a non-resident person who is not registered under Subdivision d of Division V of Part IX of the Act at the time the supply is made, to the extent that the service is in respect of a supply to that person of a freight transportation service that is included in section 6, 7, 8, 9 or 10.

PART VIII

INTERNATIONAL ORGANIZATIONS AND OFFICIALS

1. A supply of property or a service that is for the use of the Governor General.

2. A supply of property or a service to an international bridge or tunnel authority for use in the construction of a bridge or tunnel that crosses the boundary between Canada and the United States.

PART IX

FINANCIAL SERVICES

1. A supply of a financial service (other than a supply that is included in section 2) made by a financial institution to a non-resident person, except where the service relates to

(*a*) a debt that arises from

(i) the deposit of funds in Canada, where the instrument issued as evidence of the deposit is a negotiable instrument, or

(ii) the lending of money that is primarily for use in Canada;

(*b*) a debt for all or part of the consideration for a supply of real property that is situated in Canada;

(*c*) a debt for all or part of the consideration for a supply of personal property that is for use primarily in Canada;

(*d*) a debt for all or part of the consideration for a supply of a service that is to be performed primarily in Canada; or

(*e*) a transfer of ownership of a property that is a debt security, an equity security or an interest in a partnership or trust, or any right in respect of such an interest, and the financial institution is buying or selling the property as a principal (other than a transfer in respect of which the financial institution is acting in the capacity of an underwriter).

2. A supply made by a financial institution of a financial service that relates to an insurance policy issued by the institution (other than a service that relates to investments made by the institution), to the extent that

(*a*) where the policy is a life or accident and sickness insurance policy (other than group policy), it is issued in respect of an individual who at the time the policy becomes effective, is a non-resident individual;

(*b*) where the policy is a group life or accident and sickness insurance policy, it relates to non-resident individuals who are insured under the policy;

(*c*) where the policy is a policy in respect of real property, it relates to property situated outside Canada; and

(*d*) where the policy is a policy of any other kind, it relates to risks that are ordinarily situated outside Canada.

3. A supply of a financial service that is the supply of precious metals where the supply is made by the refiner thereof or by the person on whose behalf the precious metals were refined.

SCHEDULE VII
(Sections 213 and 217)

NON-TAXABLE IMPORTATIONS

1. Goods that are classified under heading No. 98.01, 98.02, 98.03, 98.04, 98.05, 98.06, 98.07, 98.10, 98.11, 98.12, 98.13, 98.14, 98.15, 98.16, 98.19 or 98.21 of Schedule 1 to the *Customs Tariff*, to the extent that the goods are not subject to duty under that Act, but not including goods that are classified under tariff item No. 9804.30.00.

2. Medals, trophies and other prizes, not including usual merchantable goods, that are won outside Canada in competitions, that are bestowed, received or accepted outside Canada or that are donated by persons outside Canada, for heroic deeds, valour or distinction.

3. Printed matter that is to be made available to the general public, without charge, for the promotion of tourism, where the printed matter is

(*a*) imported by or on the order of a foreign government or an agency or representative of a foreign government; or

(*b*) imported by a board of trade, chamber of commerce, municipal or automobile association or similar organization to which it was supplied for no consideration, other than shipping and handling charges.

4. Goods that are imported by a particular person where the goods are supplied to the particular person by a non-resident person for no consideration, other than shipping and handling charges, as replacement parts under a warranty in respect of tangible personal property.

6. Goods the supply of which is included in section 2 of Part I of or in Part II, III, IV or VIII of Schedule VI.

7. Goods (other than prescribed goods) that are sent to the recipient of the supply of the goods at an address in Canada by mail or courier and the value of which, determined under subsection 215(1) of the Act, is not more than $40.

8. Prescribed goods imported in prescribed circumstances.

INDEX